MIT

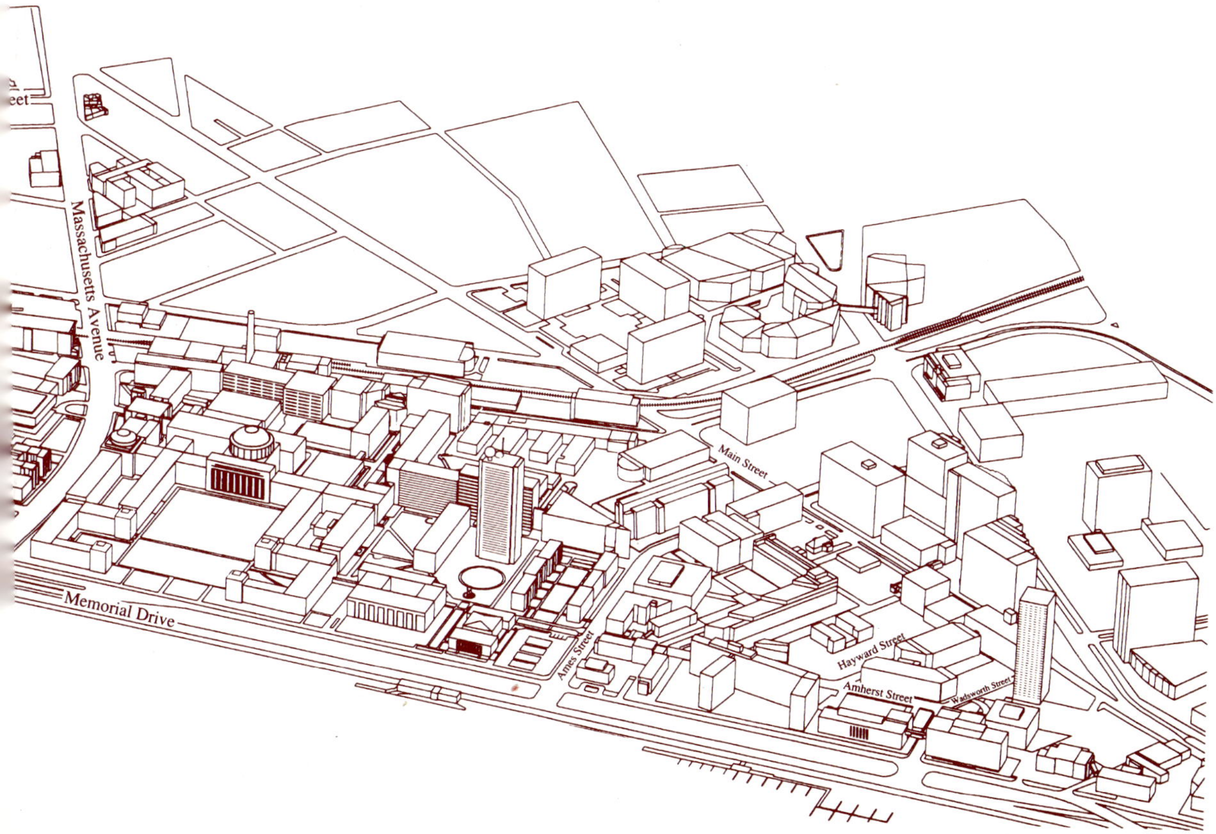
Massachusetts Avenue
Memorial Drive
Main Street
Ames Street
Hayward Street
Amherst Street
Wadsworth Street

MIT

What's Cooking Under the Dome

M I T
Women's League

MIT

Alyce McLaughlin, our cover artist, an active member of the Women's League, works in oils, watercolor and acrylic. Although she is a Boston native presently living in Bedford, Massachusetts, she spends much of her time on Cape Cod, where her favorite subjects are seascapes and lighthouses. Alyce has studied with a number of New England artists and at the Kendall Center for the Arts. Her work in oils has carried to furniture painting and canvas floor cloths. She also teaches a class in oil painting.

This cookbook is a collection of favorite recipes,
which are not necessarily original recipes.

77 Massachusetts Avenue
Cambridge, Massachusetts 02139
(617) 253-3656

Published by the MIT Women's League

ISBN: 0-9652039-0-5
Library of Congress Catalog Number: 96-85111

Edited, Designed and Manufactured by
Favorite Recipes® Press
P.O. Box 305142
Nashville, Tennessee 37230
1 (800) 358-0560

Manufactured in the United States of America
First Printing: 1996   6,500 copies

Drawings from *Sketches of the New Massachusetts Institute of Technology*
at the Dedication June 1916, Birch Burdette Long, Alumni Association,
The University Press, Cambridge

Photo Credits: Donna Coveney, *Tech Talk*, MIT
The MIT Museum
Lincoln Laboratory, MIT

The proceeds realized for the sales of
What's Cooking Under The Dome
will be donated to the
MIT Women's League Scholarship Fund.

MIT

Contents

MIT

Introduction

What's Cooking Under the Dome has been a labor of love from beginning to end. Conceived in 1992 as an offshoot of the eightieth-year celebration of the MIT Women's League, it was an idea that instantly caught the imagination of everyone who heard about it, from involved members of the League to members of the MIT community at large who leapt at the invitation to contribute their favorite recipes. Might the League have a best-seller on its hands?

We regret space did not permit us to use all the wonderful dishes that came our way. We selected the recipes to satisfy taste and appeal at varying levels of complexity, from easy and quick to more complicated and time-consuming. Many of them we (the testers and tasters) have already incorporated into our own cooking repertoires. We think you will find something here to please every palate.

All proceeds from the sale of *What's Cooking Under the Dome* go to the MIT Women's League Scholarship Fund (originally The Technology Matrons Student Aid Fund) for the benefit of undergraduate women. Typically, this translates to partial scholarships each year for two or more talented young women.

The MIT Women's League dates its informal beginning to the late 1880s, when MIT faculty and administrators' wives began meeting informally for tea and other social activities. In 1913 their association was formalized as The Technology Matrons—a name that endured until 1975, when it was changed to The MIT Women's League to reflect the changed needs and projects of its members.

Throughout their sixty-plus years, the Technology Matrons worked to help make the Institute a friendlier place, and to conduct service projects that benefited the needs and circumstances of members of the MIT community. Thus, during World War I, Matrons shipped personal comfort items (clothing, towels, books, soap) to MIT servicemen overseas. And during the 1918 flu epidemic, they contributed a total of 1,399 days of nursing care to four convalescent homes.

INTRODUCTION

In 1931, in recognition of the Institute's growing foreign student population, the Matrons formed a Foreign Student Hospitality Committee, an activity now so central to the Institute that it has been incorporated into its Office of Undergraduate Education and Student Affairs. In 1932, they established their first interest group, the Chorale, which has since grown into a thirty-five to fifty voice concert choir that meets weekly and gives several concerts a year. The Matrons/League now offers up to twenty interest groups a year—ongoing opportunities for MIT women to make new friends and share their talents and interests.

During World War II, Matrons gave recreational items (hats, dominoes, cards, books) to the American Ambulance Hospital in Paris, collected similar articles for soldiers in camps, and made surgical dressings for the Red Cross. They also staged semi-annual blood drives, yet another activity that has since been subsumed into the Institute's regular administrative responsibilities.

The Furniture Exchange (FX), where MIT students (and now Harvard, Suffolk, and BU students, as well) can buy used furniture and household accessories at affordable prices, was founded in 1958. The FX today has a paid manager, enjoys expanded quarters (after three upgrade moves) at 350 Brookline Street, and contributes—over $150,000 to date—to the MIT Women's League Scholarship Fund for undergraduate women.

Early in the 1960s, the Matrons spotted the need to welcome incoming foreign students beyond a first greeting. The expanded program matched these students with host families who not only met them on arrival, but also helped them find housing and get settled, and maintained interest in them throughout their stays at MIT. Demand increased so dramatically that (as with so many of the Matrons' earlier programs) the Hosts to International Students Program, as it is now called, is now administered by MIT.

Also in the 1960s, the Technology Matrons initiated two other activities that have since become regular features of the MIT scene: (1) English Conversation Classes for wives of international students and visiting staff, now including babysitting during class time; more than 200 international women enroll each year. (2) The Technology Nursery School in Westgate, later incorporated as a nonprofit corporation. (In 1982, the MIT Women's League, née Technology Matrons, contributed $2,000 to the Eastgate Children's Center playground.)

In 1971, the Technology Matrons' *Family Guide to MIT*, which the Matrons had updated and published every two years since 1956, was united with three other publications into an expanded *HoToGAMIT (How To Get Around MIT)*. Every year MIT updates this popular booklet and distributes it to freshmen and new graduate students. Nearly ten years later, the Matrons' popular fall foliage tours, long a mainstay of its social program, were accorded similar recognition when MIT assumed responsibility for their management and execution via the MIT Activities Committee (MITAC).

In 1994, as an outgrowth of earlier, successful health-related service projects inspired by the wife of former MIT president Julius A. Stratton, the League established the Catherine N. Stratton Fund to underwrite annual lectures on social and political issues. The Stratton lectures represent the League's continuing efforts to find the best ways to extend hospitality and friendliness to MIT students, faculty, and staff members, serve mutual interests, and serve the Institute.

In 1995, the League published *The MIT Women's League: A Rich Heritage*, an easy-to-read booklet that captures the essence of the League's origins, growth, and volunteers who have made the League a unique and remarkable organization.

The Cookbook Committee
Sis de Bordenave
Martha Harleman
Mary Hill
Elizabeth Kleiman
Alyce McLaughlin
Cleo Schimmel

MIT

Acknowledgements

The activity of compiling a community cookbook is a highly detailed and time-consuming process and would never happen without the help of many hands.

We wish to thank the numerous MIT contributors who participated either by donating their time or their recipe and those who tried, tested, tasted, advised, and encouraged the project along. Thanks also to those special friends of the MIT community who helped with the testing: Mary Jane St. Amour, Louise Bixler, Patricia Rafael, Judith Chernoff, Elizabeth Harleman, Kathleen Harleman, Mary Murray, Patricia Phillips, Jean Treat, and Anne Harleman Kreiger.

Special thanks go to Chef Peter Rhein and his associate, James Mahoney, who worked with us every step of the way in every capacity, allowing us the use of the MIT Administrative Host Kitchen.

To Bill Branch, Judy Jackson, and Favorite Recipes® Press staff who provided the framework, critical eye, and timely advice we came to rely on, we say thank you.

We are most grateful for the support of the Women's League Office and its chairman, Dee Ippen, whose endorsement and supervision were important to the success of this project. Most of all, we are indebted to Sis de Bordenave, our valued Administrative Assistant, who probably tested and tasted more recipes than anyone in the entire MIT community without losing her sense of humor or her waistline and without whose organizational skills this book would never have become a reality.

Bits and Bytes

(APPETIZERS & ACCOMPANIMENTS)

MIT
Women's League

Cream Cheese Spread

8 ounces cream cheese, softened
1/4 cup chutney
1/4 teaspoon dry mustard
1 teaspoon curry powder, or to taste
Toasted almonds to taste
Rye bread rounds
Chopped fresh parsley

Combine the cream cheese, chutney, dry mustard, curry powder and almonds in a bowl and mix well. Spread over the bread rounds. Garnish with the parsley.

You may thin this down a bit and use it as a dip.

Yields 1 1/4 to 1 1/2 cups.

Dorothy G. Adler

Eggplant Caviar

I got into the habit of preparing this dish at our summer place because of the abundance of eggplant from our garden there.

Catherine Stratton is the wife of a former MIT president.

1 large eggplant
1 clove of garlic, crushed
1 large onion, chopped
1/2 cup virgin olive oil
2 tomatoes, peeled, chopped
Salt and freshly ground pepper to taste
2 teaspoons dry white wine

Place the whole eggplant in a baking pan. Bake at 400 degrees for 1 hour or until tender.

Peel and finely chop the eggplant.

Simmer the garlic and onion in the olive oil in a skillet until tender but not browned. Stir in a mixture of the eggplant and tomatoes. Season with the salt and pepper. Stir in the wine. Cook until the mixture is thickened, stirring constantly.

Let stand to cool. Chill until serving time.

Serve ice cold with pumpernickel or silver dollar thin pieces of rye bread.

Yields 2 to 3 cups.

Catherine N. Stratton

Oyster Roll

1 can smoked oysters, drained
8 ounces cream cheese, softened
3 tablespoons mayonnaise
1 tablespoon minced fresh onion
2 tablespoons minced fresh parsley

Cut the oysters into small pieces with scissors; do not mash the oysters.

Combine the oysters, cream cheese, mayonnaise and onion in a bowl and mix well.

Shape into a roll. Chill thoroughly. Roll in the parsley.

Serve with stone ground thin wheat crackers.

Yields 20 to 30 servings.

Julia A. Kaufmann

Celery Crisp as a Cracker

Wash an Irish potato and cut it into 6 pieces. Drop into a container with the celery. Cover with water and place in the refrigerator. Old celery will freshen like magic.

Shrimp Mold

1 envelope unflavored gelatin
1/4 cup cold water
1 (10-ounce) can tomato soup
8 ounces cream cheese
1 tablespoon onion juice
1 tablespoon butter
1/2 cup mayonnaise
1/2 cup whipped cream
1/2 cup chopped olives
1 cup chopped green bell pepper
1/2 cup chopped celery
1 pound shrimp, boiled, chopped
Salt to taste
1 tablespoon Tabasco sauce, or to taste
1 tablespoon Worcestershire sauce

Soften the gelatin in the cold water.

Heat the soup in a double boiler. Add the cream cheese, onion juice and butter. Cook until heated through, stirring until smooth. Add the gelatin mixture and let cool. Add the mayonnaise, whipped cream, olives, green pepper, celery, shrimp, salt, Tabasco sauce and Worcestershire sauce and mix well.

Spoon into a wet mold or a mold greased with mayonnaise. Chill for 2 hours or longer. Unmold onto a serving plate. Freezes well.

Yields 8 to 10 servings.

Strange and Wonderful Hors d'Oeuvre

A popular Near Eastern dish we've used for years at Toby Hill, Vermont

1 small Brie cheese with skin
3 to 4 tablespoons finely chopped preserved ginger
1/4 cup toasted slivered almonds

Place the cheese in a small ovenproof pot. Sprinkle with the ginger and almonds.

Bake at 350 degrees until bubbly. Serve on French bread or Melba toast.

Yields 8 to 10 servings.

Catherine N. Stratton

Stilton and Hazelnut Spread

8 ounces Stilton cheese, crumbled, softened
4 ounces cream cheese, softened
3 tablespoons tawny port or medium-dry sherry, or to taste
Salt and pepper to taste
1/3 cup chopped toasted peeled hazelnuts

Blend the Stilton cheese, cream cheese, port, salt and pepper in a food processor. Add the hazelnuts. Process until mixed.

Place in a ramekin or crock. Chill until firm.

Garnish with additional hazelnuts. Serve with Melba toast.

Yields 2 cups.

Spicy Peanut Dip

1 3/4 cups smooth peanut butter
2 medium onions, finely chopped
6 cloves of garlic, finely chopped
6 tablespoons lemon juice
1/4 cup chopped fresh cilantro
4 teaspoons grated fresh ginger
4 teaspoons soy sauce
2 teaspoons turmeric
2 teaspoons dried red pepper flakes

Combine the peanut butter, onions, garlic, lemon juice, cilantro, ginger, soy sauce, turmeric and pepper flakes in a food processor container. Purée until smooth, adding water to thin if needed.

Serve with your favorite bite-size fresh vegetables.

Yields 2 cups.

Cheese and Pepperoni Pie

For serving ease place these squares in paper cupcake holders and arrange on a platter.

2 packages refrigerator crescent rolls
1 pound full-cream ricotta cheese
1 roll pepperoni, peeled, chopped
1 egg, beaten
3/4 cup shredded Swiss cheese
1/4 teaspoon onion powder
1/2 teaspoon dried oregano
1/4 teaspoon pepper

Spray the bottom and sides of a 9x12-inch baking pan with nonstick cooking spray. Spread 1 package of the rolls in the pan, pressing to seal the perforations. Bake, covered with foil, at 350 degrees for 15 minutes. Cool for 5 minutes.

Combine the ricotta cheese, pepperoni, egg, Swiss cheese, onion powder, oregano and pepper in a bowl. Spread over the baked layer. Top with the remaining rolls, sealing the perforations and spreading the dough to the edges of the pan. Bake, uncovered, at 350 degrees or until golden brown. Cool for 15 minutes or longer. Cut into small squares.

Yields 12 servings.

Deanne Sferrino

Cheese Straws

A good way to use up cheese and a leftover egg yolk

3/4 cup flour
1/4 teaspoon salt
1/8 teaspoon dry mustard, or to taste
6 tablespoons butter or margarine, chopped
3 ounces sharp Cheddar cheese, shredded
1 egg yolk
2 tablespoons (about) cold water

Sift the flour, salt and mustard into a bowl. Cut in the butter until crumbly. Stir in the cheese. Add a mixture of the egg yolk and water, stirring until a soft sticky dough forms. Let stand until the dough has relaxed a bit.

Roll 1/4 inch thick on a floured surface. Cut into 1/2x6-inch strips. Twist the strips and arrange on a floured baking sheet.

Bake at 425 degrees for 5 minutes. Cool on a wire rack.

Yields 1 1/2 to 2 dozen.

Maureen Miller

Chinese Chicken Wings

24 chicken wingettes
10 tablespoons soy sauce
1 cup packed light brown sugar
1 tablespoon garlic salt
1 teaspoon ginger

Rinse the chicken and pat dry.

Mix the soy sauce, brown sugar, garlic salt and ginger in a bowl. Add the chicken, stirring to coat evenly. Marinate in the refrigerator for 5 to 6 hours.

Remove the chicken from the marinade, shaking to remove the excess. Arrange in a foil-lined 10x15-inch baking pan. Bake at 375 degrees for 40 minutes, turning once.

Yields 8 servings.

Barbara Keicher

Green Grape Parsley Relish

1 cup seedless green grapes, cut into halves
1/4 cup red wine vinegar
1/4 cup virgin olive oil
1 teaspoon minced garlic
1/4 cup chopped parsley
Salt and pepper to taste

Mix the grapes, vinegar, olive oil, garlic, parsley, salt and pepper in a bowl.

Serve with grilled fish or poultry. Store leftovers in the refrigerator.

Yields 1 1/2 to 2 cups.

Crostini with Ricotta, Prosciutto and Basil Spread

Baguettes, cut into 1/4-inch slices
Extra-virgin olive oil
1/2 cup mild olive oil
1/2 cup coarsely chopped garlic
8 ounces thinly sliced prosciutto, cut into 1/4-inch cubes
2 pounds fresh ricotta cheese
1 cup finely chopped fresh basil or flat leaf parsley
1 tablespoon coarsely ground pepper

Arrange the bread slices on a large baking sheet. Brush with the extra-virgin olive oil. Bake at 350 degrees for 15 minutes or until toasted.

Warm the mild olive oil in a medium heavy skillet over low heat. Increase the heat to moderate. Add the garlic. Cook for 6 minutes or until golden, stirring frequently. Add the prosciutto. Cook for 2 to 3 minutes or until the prosciutto begins to change color. Remove from the heat.

Place the cheese in a large bowl. Add the prosciutto mixture with a slotted spoon and mix well. Cover and chill thoroughly. Let stand until mixture is room temperature. Stir in the basil and pepper. Spoon into bowls.

Serve with the crostini and crudités.

If fresh ricotta cheese is not available, use 2 1/2 pounds from the supermarket and drain it in a fine sieve for several hours before using.

Yields 6 cups spread.

Glenda Tabaczynski

Hot and Spicy Eggplant

3 (1-pound) eggplant
3 large onions, chopped
2 to 4 tablespoons light olive oil
3 large sweet peppers, any combination of colors, sliced
1 hot pepper, chopped, or to taste
1/4 cup grated fresh ginger, or to taste
1 teaspoon sweet Hungarian paprika
1 1/2 cups chopped tomatoes
Salt and pepper to taste

Place the eggplant in a baking pan. Bake at 450 degrees for 30 minutes or until collapsed. Let cool. Scoop the pulp from the eggplant into a bowl, discarding the skin.

Sauté the onions in the oil in a heavy skillet for 10 minutes. Add the pepper slices and chopped pepper. Sauté for 5 minutes. Add the eggplant, ginger and paprika. Cook for 1 to 2 minutes, stirring constantly. Add the tomatoes, salt and pepper. Cook for 10 to 15 minutes or until the vegetables are tender.

Yields 10 servings.

Liba Mikic

Seasoned Pita Chips

These chips are good as a nice accompaniment to the eggplant dip or may stand alone.

2/3 cup butter, softened
1/3 cup olive oil
Pepper and garlic powder to taste
Oregano and thyme to taste
Crumbled feta cheese to taste
8 slices Syrian bread, split into 2 pieces

Mix the butter, olive oil, pepper, garlic powder, oregano, thyme and cheese in a bowl. Spread over the bread. Cut each circle into small wedges. Arrange on a baking sheet.

Bake at 350 degrees for 5 to 10 minutes or until crisp.

Yields 8 servings.

Stuffed Eggplant Roll Cosmo

Chef Louis Ferretti consulted for MIT for many prestigious events on campus, including President Vest's inauguration, Technology Day, the Biology Building Dedication, the Women's League Gala, and many more.

1 large eggplant
1 egg
1 egg white
1/4 cup olive oil
1 cup ricotta cheese
1/2 cup shredded mozzarella cheese
1/4 cup freshly grated Parmesan cheese
2 tablespoons chopped fresh parsley
2 tablespoons chopped fresh basil, or 1 teaspoon dried
1 egg yolk
4 thin slices prosciutto
2 cups whipping cream
3/4 teaspoon minced garlic
2 tablespoons dry white wine
1/3 cup freshly grated Parmesan cheese
1/8 teaspoon salt
1/8 teaspoon ground white pepper
3 tablespoons cold butter, cut into chunks

Peel the eggplant and trim the stem end. Cut lengthwise into 1/4-inch-thick slices. Select 8 large slices, reserving any remaining slices for another use. Beat the egg and egg white in a pie plate. Heat 2 tablespoons of the olive oil in a large skillet over medium-high heat. Dip the eggplant slices in the egg mixture. Drain briefly and place in the skillet without crowding. Cook for 3 minutes per side or until golden brown and fork-tender. Drain on paper towels. Repeat the cooking process until all the slices are used, adding more oil 1 tablespoon at a time as needed.

For the filling, combine the ricotta cheese, mozzarella cheese, 1/4 cup Parmesan cheese, parsley, basil and egg yolk in a bowl and mix well. Spread 2 tablespoons of the filling across the stem end of each eggplant slice. Cut the prosciutto slices into halves lengthwise. Place 1 strip over the filling on each slice. Roll up the eggplant from the narrow end. Place seam side down in 8 individual ramekins or in a 9x13-inch baking dish.

For the sauce, bring the whipping cream to a boil in a heavy 2-quart saucepan. Cook over medium heat until reduced to 1 cup. Remove from the heat. Add the garlic, wine, 1/3 cup Parmesan cheese, salt and pepper. Add the butter, stirring until melted. Let cool.

Cover the eggplant with the sauce. Bake, covered, at 350 degrees for 20 minutes or until heated through and bubbly. Garnish each serving with fresh basil leaves and red and yellow bell pepper strips.

Yields 8 servings.

Louis Ferretti

Honey Curry Appetizers

1 cup dry white wine
1 tablespoon curry
1 tablespoon honey
3/4 to 1 cup mayonnaise

Bring the wine, curry and honey to a boil in a small nonreactive saucepan, stirring constantly. Cook until reduced to 1/4 cup. Let cool. Stir in the mayonnaise. Chill, covered, until serving time.

You may use this as a dip if serving it with cold cooked shrimp or snow peas. Dab it on and beside cold cooked asparagus or spread decoratively over hard-cooked egg halves. You may arrange decoratively over lettuce on individual plates.

You may roll 2 to 3 spears of cooked asparagus in thin individual omelets, roll them up and top them with a dollop of the mayonnaise mixture.

Yield is variable.

Paula Brody

Cocktail Meatballs

2 pounds ground round or ground turkey
1 cup cornflake crumbs
2 tablespoons soy sauce
2 eggs
1/4 teaspoon pepper
1/4 teaspoon parsley
1/2 teaspoon garlic powder
1/3 cup catsup
2 tablespoons minced onion
1 (16-ounce) can jellied cranberry sauce
1 (12-ounce) bottle chili sauce
2 tablespoons dark brown sugar
1 tablespoon lemon juice

Combine the ground round, cornflake crumbs, soy sauce, eggs, pepper, parsley, garlic powder, catsup and onion in a bowl and mix well. Shape into small balls and place in a 10x15-inch baking pan.

Combine the cranberry sauce, chili sauce, brown sugar and lemon juice in a saucepan. Cook until the cranberry sauce is melted, stirring frequently. Pour over the meatballs.

Bake at 350 degrees for 30 minutes.

These may be frozen after baking. Reheat to serve.

Yields 65 to 70 meatballs.

Martha R. Jennings

Sherried Mushroom Strudel

¼ cup unsalted butter
6 cups minced mushrooms
Salt to taste
1 teaspoon curry powder
6 tablespoons sherry
¼ cup chopped shallots
1 cup sour cream
3 tablespoons bread crumbs
8 sheets phyllo dough
½ cup melted unsalted butter
1 cup bread crumbs

Melt ¼ cup butter in a skillet over medium-low heat.

Add the mushrooms, salt, curry powder, sherry and shallots. Sauté for 20 minutes or until the mushrooms are wilted and the liquid is evaporated. Let cool.

Stir in the sour cream and 3 tablespoons bread crumbs. Chill overnight.

Brush 1 sheet of phyllo with a small amount of melted butter and sprinkle with a few bread crumbs. Repeat until there are 4 layers.

Spread half the mushroom mixture over the phyllo, leaving a 1-inch border. Roll as for a jelly roll. Brush with melted butter and sprinkle with bread crumbs. Place on a lightly greased baking sheet.

Score the roll into 8 slices using a sharp knife.

Repeat the above process with the remaining phyllo and mushroom mixture.

Bake at 375 degrees for 40 minutes or until browned.

Garnish each serving with a dollop of sour cream and chopped scallions.

Yields 16 servings.

Ellen Shapiro

Mushroom Turnovers

9 ounces cream cheese, softened
$1/2$ cup unsalted butter, softened
$1\,1/2$ cups flour, sifted
1 large onion, finely chopped
8 ounces mushrooms, finely chopped
1 small carrot, chopped
3 tablespoons unsalted butter
1 tablespoon sherry
1 tablespoon finely chopped parsley
$1/2$ teaspoon thyme
2 tablespoons flour
$1/4$ cup sour cream

Combine the cream cheese, $1/2$ cup butter and $1\,1/2$ cups flour in a bowl. Mix with a pastry blender until a smooth dough forms. Chill for 30 minutes or longer.

Combine the onion, mushrooms, carrot and 3 tablespoons butter in a skillet. Sauté over low heat for 10 minutes or until the vegetables are tender but not browned. Add the sherry, parsley, thyme and 2 tablespoons flour. Cook for 5 minutes. Remove from the heat and let cool. Stir in the sour cream.

Roll the dough $1/8$ inch thick on a lightly floured surface. Cut with a 3-inch cookie cutter. Place 1 teaspoon of the mushroom mixture on each round. Fold the dough in half over the filling, pressing the edges with a fork to seal. Prick the top of each turnover 3 times. Place on a nonstick baking sheet.

Bake at 400 to 425 degrees for 15 minutes or until lightly browned. If the filling begins to leak, turn the turnover over and reseal the edges with a fork.

Yields 18 to 20 servings.

Jarmila Z. Jhrbek

New Potatoes with Caviar

I first had this hors d'oeuvre at a party in the hills overlooking San Francisco and the Golden Gate Bridge—a spectacular setting deserving of spectacular food. The view met its match in this one.

12 very small red new potatoes
Rock salt
1 package crème fraîche
1 small jar black caviar
1 bunch fresh chives, finely chopped

Wipe off the potatoes and place in an 11x15-inch baking dish. Cover completely with rock salt. Roast at 425 degrees for 40 minutes. Remove the potatoes from the salt. Split each potato into halves. Top each half with a dollop of crème fraîche, a small amount of caviar and a sprinkling of chives.

Arrange on a tray. Serve immediately with Champagne.

Yields 8 servings.

Kathryn A. Willmore

Mother Leone's Shrimp Sauce

2 scallions, chopped
6 tablespoons finely chopped green bell pepper
1 tablespoon grated sweet onion
2 tablespoons chopped capers
1 clove of garlic, crushed
1/2 cup chili sauce
1/2 teaspoon salt
1/2 teaspoon crushed red pepper
1/2 teaspoon black pepper
2 tablespoons horseradish
1 cup mayonnaise
5 pounds fresh cocktail shrimp, cooked, peeled

Drain the scallions, green pepper, onion and capers through a fine strainer or cheesecloth. Combine the garlic, chili sauce, salt, red pepper, black pepper, horseradish and mayonnaise in a bowl and mix well. Stir in the drained ingredients. Add the shrimp. Marinate in the refrigerator overnight.

Remove the shrimp to a large bowl with a slotted spoon.

Yields 20 to 30 servings.

Phyllis E. Reservitz

Shrimp in Mustard Sauce

2 1/4 pounds shrimp
1/2 cup finely chopped parsley
1/2 cup finely chopped green onions
1/4 cup tarragon vinegar
3/4 cup wine vinegar
1/4 cup olive oil
5 tablespoons Dijon mustard
2 tablespoons crushed red pepper
2 teaspoons salt
2 teaspoons freshly ground black pepper

Cook the shrimp in boiling water to cover in a large pot until pink. Drain, peel and devein the shrimp. Place in a large bowl.

Mix the parsley, green onions, tarragon vinegar, wine vinegar, olive oil, Dijon mustard, red pepper, salt and black pepper in a medium bowl. Pour over the warm shrimp, stirring to coat. Cover and marinate in the refrigerator overnight.

Serve with crackers.

Yields 6 to 8 servings.

Richard Hill

Tuna Devils

Many ideas could be used in connection with this recipe; for example, tiny pastries could be filled with the tuna mixture.

1 can tuna, drained, flaked
3 tablespoons chopped onion
1 tablespoon Worcestershire sauce
Tabasco sauce to taste
1/3 cup mayonnaise
1 cup soft bread crumbs
4 scallop shells
Grated Parmesan cheese
Olive oil
Paprika to taste

Mix the tuna, onion, Worcestershire sauce, Tabasco sauce and mayonnaise in a bowl. Add the bread crumbs, stirring to coat. Spoon into the scallop shells. Top generously with the cheese. Drizzle with a small amount of olive oil. Sprinkle with the paprika. Place on a baking sheet.

Bake at 350 degrees for 20 minutes.

Yields 4 servings.

Ruth Milne

Cranberry, Pear and Apple Chutney

This is wonderful with a turkey dinner or cold turkey sandwiches.

2 cups cranberries
2 cups coarsely chopped peeled apples
2 cups coarsely chopped peeled pears
1 1/2 cups packed light brown sugar
1/2 cup raisins
1 1/2 cups water
1/2 cup cider vinegar
1 teaspoon ground ginger
1 teaspoon ground allspice
3/4 teaspoon ground cloves

Combine the cranberries, apples, pears, brown sugar, raisins, water, vinegar, ginger, allspice and cloves in a large pot. Bring to a gentle boil over medium-high heat, stirring occasionally; reduce the heat. Simmer for 35 minutes or until the fruit is tender and the mixture is the consistency of salsa, stirring occasionally at first and more frequently toward the end of the cooking time. Add additional water if needed to maintain consistency. Let cool. Cover and store in the refrigerator.

Yields 4 cups.

Dorothy A. Mark

Granola

4 cups old-fashioned oats
2/3 cup unsweetened wheat germ
1/2 cup sesame seeds
1/2 cup sunflower seeds
1/2 cup chopped pecans
1/4 cup almonds, pine nuts or pumpkin seeds
1/2 cup packed brown sugar, honey or maple syrup
1/2 teaspoon salt
1 tablespoon vanilla extract
1/4 cup vegetable oil
1/4 cup water
1 cup raisins or dates

Combine the oats, wheat germ, sesame seeds, sunflower seeds, pecans, almonds, brown sugar, salt and vanilla in a large bowl and mix well. Shake the oil with the water in a covered jar until mixed. Stir into the oat mixture. Spread 1/2 inch thick or less in a large baking pan.

Bake at 325 degrees for 30 minutes or until the oats are a toast color, stirring every 10 minutes. Stir in the raisins. Bake for 3 minutes longer.

Let cool. Store in an airtight container.

Yields 7 to 8 cups.

Alice Huang and David Baltimore

Spiced Apricots

A glamorous pickle adds much color and flavor to a meal. This is a basic recipe for spice syrup to which you can add any fruit; for example, peaches, apples, or pears. Dried fruit needs to be soaked overnight.

Dried apricots or prunes
1 cinnamon stick
2 tablespoons whole cloves
2 tablespoons allspice berries
4 cups sugar
2 cups water
2 cups cider vinegar
1 lemon, thinly sliced

Soak the apricots in water to cover overnight.

Crush the cinnamon stick and measure 2 tablespoons cinnamon. Place the cinnamon, cloves and allspice in a cheesecloth bag and tie with a string.

Combine the sugar, 2 cups water and vinegar in a large pot. Add the lemon and spice bag. Simmer for 45 minutes or until the mixture is syrupy.

Drain the apricots and add to the syrup. Cook for 10 minutes or until the fruit is glazed.

Remove from the heat. Pour into hot sterilized jars, leaving 1/2 inch headspace; seal with 2-piece lids.

The syrup may be prepared ahead and stored in a cool place or the refrigerator for several weeks. The spice bag may be reused with fresh spices.

Yield is variable.

Catherine N. Stratton

Green Tomato Relish

Several years ago, my husband and I had an audience with the emperor and empress of Japan. A Japanese friend suggested we take them some of this relish. The emperor loved it, and the empress wrote me asking for the recipe. The recipe comes from my grandmother.

Priscilla Gray is the wife of a former MIT President.

2 1/2 quarts green tomatoes, sliced
1/4 cup salt
4 cups cider vinegar
3 cups sugar
1 teaspoon turmeric
1 teaspoon celery seeds
2 tablespoons mustard seeds
2 quarts onions, sliced
2 red bell peppers, chopped
1 red hot pepper, chopped

Sprinkle the tomatoes with the salt. Let stand overnight and drain well.

Combine the vinegar, sugar, turmeric, celery seeds and mustard seeds in a large pot. Bring to a boil. Add the onions, tomatoes and peppers. Return to a boil. Boil for 10 minutes.

Pour into hot sterilized jars, leaving 1/2 inch headspace; seal with 2-piece lids.

Yields 4 to 5 quarts.

Priscilla K. Gray

Mary Bedogian's Salsa

1 large tomato or 2 small tomatoes
4 scallions, finely chopped
1 (4-ounce) can chopped black olives
1 (4-ounce) can chopped green chiles
2 tablespoons red wine vinegar
1 teaspoon olive oil (optional)
1/8 teaspoon Tabasco sauce, or to taste
1/8 teaspoon cayenne, or to taste

Chop the tomato, reserving the juice. Combine the tomato, tomato juice, scallions, olives, green chiles, vinegar, olive oil, Tabasco sauce and cayenne in a bowl and mix well.

Serve with tortilla chips.

Yields 2 to 3 cups.

Chesley T. Logcher

Leavenings and Elevenses

(Breads & Brunches)

MIT
Women's League

Cheese Biscuits

We measure out the dry ingredients into sandwich bags for six extensions or more so that we can make biscuits at a moment's notice.

2 cups flour
1 tablespoon sugar
4 teaspoons baking powder
1/2 teaspoon cream of tartar
1 teaspoon salt
1/8 teaspoon cayenne, or to taste
1/2 cup cold butter, cut into pieces
1 cup shredded sharp cheese
1 cup (about) milk

Combine the flour, sugar, baking powder, cream of tartar, salt and cayenne in a food processor container. Add the butter, processing until the mixture resembles cornmeal. Add the cheese. Add the milk with the food processor running, processing until a ball forms.

Press into a circle 1/2 inch thick on a floured surface. Cut with a biscuit cutter. Place biscuits close together on a greased baking sheet. Bake at 375 degrees for 20 minutes.

Yields 1 dozen.

James Mahoney

Sweet Cinnamon Yeast Rolls

1 cup butter, softened
2 tablespoons sugar
3 egg yolks
1 cake of yeast
1/2 cup warm milk
2 cups flour
1/8 teaspoon salt, or to taste
3 egg whites
1/2 cup sugar
2 teaspoons cinnamon
1/2 cup sugar
1 cup chopped walnuts

Cream the butter and 2 tablespoons sugar in a mixer bowl until light and fluffy. Beat in the egg yolks. Dissolve the yeast in the milk. Mix the flour and salt together. Add the yeast mixture and flour mixture alternately to the creamed mixture, beating well after each addition. Chill overnight.

Beat the egg whites and 1/2 cup sugar in a mixer bowl until stiff peaks form. Mix the cinnamon, 1/2 cup sugar and walnuts together.

Divide the dough into 3 portions. Roll each portion on a floured surface. Spread with the meringue. Top with some of the walnut mixture. Roll as for a jelly roll. Place on a nonstick baking sheet. Sprinkle with the remaining walnut mixture.

Bake at 350 degrees for 40 minutes. Cut diagonally into slices.

Yields 3 dozen.

Maureen Feldman

Simple Sweet Scones

2½ cups flour
⅓ cup sugar
1 tablespoon baking powder
½ teaspoon salt
½ teaspoon nutmeg
½ cup butter
⅔ cup (or more) milk
1 cup raisins or dried cranberries, or ½ cup raisins plus ½ cup dried cranberries

Combine the flour, sugar, baking powder, salt and nutmeg in a food processor container. Cut in the butter until crumbly. Add the milk and raisins, pulsing until a soft dough forms.

Knead 3 to 4 times on a floured board. Roll or pat ½ inch thick. Cut with a round cutter or cut into squares and then triangles. Place close together but not touching on a baking sheet sprayed with nonstick cooking spray.

Bake at 425 degrees for 12 minutes. Serve warm.

Yields 1 dozen.

Making a Perfect Muffin

When making muffins, do not overmix the batter, as this will over-activate the gluten in the flour and make the muffins tough. Mix the batter just until it is moistened; there may be flecks of flour, but you will get a tender muffin.

Sour Cream Coffee Cake

2 cups flour
1 teaspoon baking powder
¼ teaspoon salt
2 tablespoons sugar
1 teaspoon cinnamon
1 cup chopped pecans
1 cup butter, softened
2 cups sugar
2 eggs
1 cup sour cream
1 tablespoon vanilla extract

Sift the flour, baking powder and salt together. Mix 2 tablespoons sugar, cinnamon and pecans together.

Cream the butter in a mixer bowl. Add 2 cups sugar gradually, beating until light and fluffy. Beat in the eggs 1 at a time. Fold in the sour cream and vanilla. Add the flour mixture and mix well.

Pour ⅓ of the batter into a greased and floured bundt pan. Sprinkle with ¾ of the pecan mixture. Spread the remaining batter in the pan and sprinkle with the remaining pecan mixture.

Bake at 350 degrees for 1 hour or until a wooden pick inserted in the coffee cake comes out clean.

Yields 12 servings.

Dee Ippen

Corn Madeleines with Thyme

3/4 cup unbleached flour
1/4 cup corn flour
1 teaspoon salt
1 teaspoon baking powder
4 eggs
Grated zest of 1 lemon
1 teaspoon finely chopped fresh thyme
1/2 cup melted unsalted butter

Sift the unbleached flour, corn flour, salt and baking powder together.

Whisk the eggs in a bowl until light and foamy. Stir in the lemon zest and thyme. Add the flour mixture 1/2 at a time, stirring after each addition. Fold in the butter. Chill for 30 minutes.

Fill buttered and floured molds 2/3 full with batter. Bake at 450 degrees for 5 minutes. Reduce the oven temperature to 400 degrees. Bake for 5 minutes or until golden brown.

Yields 2 dozen.

Revitalizing Breads

Place less-than-fresh bread in a non-recycled brown paper bag. Sprinkle with water and place in a moderate oven. This really revives bread and is ecologically friendly, since aluminum foil is not used.

Blue Ribbon Blueberry Muffins

I have many wild blueberry bushes growing in my backyard and neighborhood. Every year I pick what I need and the birds get the rest. I experimented with muffin recipes until I found the right combination of ingredients. I have received many compliments on these muffins, including from some of the MIT parking garage attendants, who got some just for being such nice guys.

1 egg
1 cup milk
1/4 cup light olive oil
1 cup flour
1/2 cup rolled oats
1/2 cup sugar
1 tablespoon baking powder
1 teaspoon salt
2 cups wild blueberries
Confectioners' sugar

Beat the egg in a bowl. Stir in the milk and olive oil. Add the flour, oats, sugar, baking powder and salt, stirring just until moistened; the batter will be lumpy. Stir in the blueberries; there will appear to be more blueberries than batter.

Fill greased 2 3/4-inch muffin cups 2/3 full. Bake at 400 degrees for 20 to 25 minutes or until golden brown. Remove from the pan immediately. Dust with confectioners' sugar.

You may mix raspberries or blackberries with the blueberries. These muffins freeze well.

Yields 1 dozen.

Kathy J. Davis

Foccacia

2 pounds cherry tomatoes, chopped
2 bunches scallions, chopped
1 head escarole, chopped
Anchovies (optional)
Grated Romano cheese to taste
Mozzarella cheese to taste
1/2 cup olive oil
Salt and pepper to taste
Oregano to taste
Pizza dough

Combine the cherry tomatoes, scallions, escarole, anchovies, Romano cheese, mozzarella cheese, olive oil, salt, pepper and oregano in a bowl and mix well. Roll the pizza dough fairly thin on a floured surface. Spread with the tomato mixture. Fold flat as for a turnover.

Brown on both sides in a small amount of olive oil in an 8-inch nonstick skillet. Drain on paper towels.

Yields 10 servings.

Laura Capone

O'Malley's Irish Bread

This recipe comes from County Cork, Ireland. When my aunts watched my grandmother make this bread, she never measured. Before she passed on, they sat down with her and measured everything. Remember to use fresh baking powder; it makes a world of difference.

Raisins to taste
3 cups flour
3/4 cup sugar
6 tablespoons baking powder
Caraway seeds to taste
6 tablespoons butter, softened
1 cup (about) buttermilk

Boil the raisins in water to cover in a saucepan for 5 minutes or until softened.

Mix the flour, sugar, baking powder and caraway seeds in a bowl. Drain the raisins and stir into the flour mixture. Cut in the butter with 2 knives until crumbly. Add the buttermilk, stirring until a soft dough forms. Knead on a floured surface until slightly sticky.

Place the dough in a buttered cast-iron skillet. Bake, covered with foil, at 350 degrees for 15 minutes. Bake, uncovered, for 30 minutes or until golden brown and a wooden pick inserted in the center comes out clean.

Invert onto a wire rack to cool. Spread the bread generously with butter.

You may also use this recipe for making scones. Drop dough the size of your palm onto a buttered baking sheet and bake until golden brown.

Yields 8 to 12 servings.

Brenda Blais

Sourdough White Bread

9 cups white flour
6 cups water
½ cup Sourdough Starter
1½ teaspoons baking soda
2 tablespoons salt
1 tablespoon sugar
5 tablespoons vegetable oil
7½ cups white flour

Mix 9 cups flour, water and Sourdough Starter in a large stainless steel or enamel pot. Cover and let stand in a warm place for 18 to 24 hours.

Remove ½ cup of the fermented mixture (the new starter) and store, loosely covered, in the refrigerator.

Combine the baking soda, salt, sugar and oil with the remaining starter in the large pot and mix well. Add 7½ cups flour gradually and knead in the pot for 10 minutes or until a soft dough forms.

Shape into 4 equal loaves in well-greased bread pans. Place a pan of water on the bottom oven rack. Heat the oven to 150 degrees; turn off the oven. Place the bread in the warm oven. Let rise for 1½ to 2 hours or until 2 to 3 times its original volume.

Bake at 350 degrees for 1 hour or until the top crust starts to brown. For a softer crust, brush with margarine at this point. Increase the oven temperature to 400 degrees. Bake for 15 to 20 minutes or until brown.

Cool on wire racks. Slice and eat as much as you can with butter or margarine.

The bread keeps well at room temperature for 3 to 4 days. Slice and freeze what won't be used right away.

Yields 4 loaves.

Sourdough Starter

The best way to obtain a starter is to ask a friend who has been maintaining one for years (like Hal). However, if you need to make your own, here's how.

1 cup white flour
1 cup water
¼ teaspoon dry yeast

Combine the flour, water and yeast in a large glass container. Let stand, loosely covered, for 1 week; after that, the starter should be refrigerated.

Follow the bread recipe directions for using and saving the starter. Wash and dry the starter container while the bread batter is fermenting.

Use the starter regularly. If unused for a month, feed the yeast with ¼ cup flour and ¼ cup water.

Yields 1 starter.

Harold M. Heggestad

Savory Crepes with Vegetable Filling and Herb Sauce

$^2/_3$ cup flour
1 cup milk
$^1/_8$ teaspoon salt, or to taste
4 eggs
2 tablespoons grated Parmesan cheese
1 teaspoon dried parsley
2 teaspoons dried chives
1 tablespoon olive oil
2 cups finely chopped mushrooms
2 cups finely chopped zucchini
$^1/_2$ teaspoon dried basil
$^1/_2$ teaspoon salt
1 $^1/_2$ tablespoons butter
1 $^1/_2$ tablespoons flour
1 $^1/_2$ cups milk
$^1/_8$ teaspoon onion powder, or to taste
$^1/_8$ teaspoon thyme, or to taste
$^1/_8$ teaspoon salt, or to taste

For the crepes, combine $^2/_3$ cup flour, 1 cup milk, $^1/_8$ teaspoon salt, eggs, Parmesan cheese, parsley and chives in a bowl and mix well.

Oil lightly a 10-inch nonstick skillet. Heat over medium-high heat. Pour in $^1/_3$ cup batter, tilting to cover the surface. Cook until the top is almost set. Loosen the edges with a narrow spatula and turn. Cook until golden brown. Remove to a plate and keep warm. Repeat with the remaining batter, oiling the skillet after every 2 crepes.

For the filling, heat 1 tablespoon olive oil in the skillet. Add the mushrooms, zucchini, basil and $^1/_2$ teaspoon salt. Sauté over medium heat.

For the sauce, melt the butter in a 1-quart saucepan. Whisk in 1 $^1/_2$ tablespoons flour. Cook for 1 to 2 minutes, whisking until smooth. Add 1 $^1/_2$ cups milk very gradually, whisking constantly; the mixture will clump at the beginning but will become smooth. Bring to a boil. Add the onion powder, thyme and $^1/_8$ teaspoon salt. Cook for several minutes, whisking frequently.

Place $^1/_3$ cup of the filling on each crepe and roll up. Pour the sauce over the crepes before serving.

Yields 4 servings.

Catherine Liddell

Cambridge Pancakes

1 cup unbleached flour
1 cup white wheat flour or cracked wheat flour
1 teaspoon baking powder
1 1/4 cups milk
1 egg
1 tablespoon canola oil
1/4 cup golden raisins
1/3 cup chopped walnuts

Mix the unbleached flour, wheat flour and baking powder in a bowl. Add the milk, egg and oil and mix well. Stir in the raisins and walnuts.

Drop by large spoonfuls into a lightly oiled nonstick skillet. Cook over medium heat until set and browned.

Serve with maple syrup.

Yields 4 servings.

Ruth Milne

Becky's Puff Pancake

Rebecca Vest is the wife of the president of MIT.

6 eggs
1 cup milk
1 cup flour
1/2 cup butter or margarine
Juice of 1 lemon
Confectioners' sugar to taste

Mix the eggs, milk and flour in a bowl; the batter will be lumpy. Melt the butter in a 9x13-inch glass baking dish. Pour the batter into the prepared dish.

Bake at 400 degrees for 20 minutes. Sprinkle with the lemon juice and confectioners' sugar.

Serve with lemon wedges and additional confectioners' sugar.

Yields 8 to 12 servings.

Rebecca M. Vest

Raised Waffles

1 package dry yeast
1/4 cup hot (105 to 115 degrees) water
1 3/4 cups milk
2 tablespoons sugar
1 teaspoon salt
3 eggs
1/4 cup melted butter
2 cups flour

Dissolve the yeast in the hot water and set aside. Scald the milk in a small saucepan. Stir in the sugar and salt. Set aside to cool.

Beat the eggs in a small bowl. Stir in the milk mixture.

Combine the yeast mixture, milk mixture and butter in a large bowl and mix well. Add the flour 1/2 cup at a time, mixing well after each addition. Let rise, covered with plastic, for 1 1/2 hours; stir well. Chill, covered, overnight. Stir again.

Cook on a waffle iron using the manufacturer's directions.

Yields 6 servings.

Bette Ritz

Italian Zucchini Crescent Pie

Served with sliced cold meats, this is excellent for a luncheon buffet.

4 cups thinly sliced zucchini
1 cup chopped onions
2 tablespoons margarine or butter
2 tablespoons parsley flakes
1/2 teaspoon salt
1/2 teaspoon pepper
1/4 teaspoon garlic powder
1/4 teaspoon basil leaves
1/4 teaspoon oregano leaves
2 eggs, beaten
2 cups shredded Muenster cheese or mozzarella cheese
1 (8-count) can refrigerator crescent rolls
2 teaspoons prepared mustard

Cook the zucchini and onion in the margarine in a large skillet for 8 minutes or until tender. Stir in the parsley flakes, salt, pepper, garlic powder, basil and oregano. Mix the eggs and cheese in a large bowl. Stir in the vegetable mixture.

Separate the crescent roll dough into 8 triangles or 2 long rectangles. Press over the bottom and up the side of a nonstick 10-inch pie plate, 8x12-inch baking dish or 11-inch quiche pan, sealing the perforations. Spread with the mustard. Pour in the egg mixture.

Bake at 375 degrees for 18 to 22 minutes or until a knife inserted near the center comes out clean. Cover the edge of the crust with foil during the last 10 minutes of baking time if needed to prevent excessive browning. Let stand for 10 minutes.

Yields 6 servings.

Eva Roos

Mushroom Cheese Tart

I first made this mushroom tart for our Boston Mycological Club Culinary Meeting in 1973; I made a large Greek version in a 9x15-inch pan in 1979. Both were well received. If you know and like wild mushrooms, most meaty, mild-tasting safe mushrooms work well.

Shirley McGowan was Administrative Host to the President's Office preceding Peter Rhein.

1 recipe (1-crust) pie pastry
2 cups chopped onions
2 teaspoons olive oil
1 1/2 pounds fresh mushrooms, sliced
1 tablespoon Worcestershire sauce
2 tablespoons fresh lemon juice
1/8 teaspoon pepper
Tabasco sauce to taste
1 cup grated Jarlsberg cheese
1/2 cup chopped fresh parsley
Salt to taste
1/2 cup grated Jarlsberg cheese
1/4 cup chopped fresh parsley

Roll out the pastry and fit into a 10- to 11-inch tart pan. Turn under the edges, pressing against the pan. Cover with plastic and chill until needed.

Sauté the onions in the olive oil in a skillet until tender. Remove with a slotted spoon to a 3-quart bowl. Sauté the mushrooms in the skillet until tender and almost dry. Combine with the onions. Add the Worcestershire sauce, lemon juice, pepper and Tabasco sauce and mix well. Let cool. Stir in 1 cup cheese and 1/2 cup parsley. Season with the salt.

Sprinkle 1/2 cup cheese in the tart shell. Top with the mushroom mixture. Sprinkle with 1/4 cup parsley.

Place in a 425-degree oven. Reduce the oven temperature to 350 degrees. Bake for 40 minutes or until the crust is golden brown.

You may use 7 sheets of phyllo dough instead of the pastry shell. Spray each sheet lightly with nonstick cooking spray. Substitute 2 tablespoons chopped fresh dill for the Worcestershire sauce and lemon juice; substitute 1/2 cup feta cheese for 1/2 cup Jarlsberg cheese.

Yields 8 servings.

Shirley R. McGowan

Cleaning Mushrooms

Never soak mushrooms, as they are porous and tend to absorb the water. Simply wipe them off with a damp cloth; cut off the stem if it is woody or tough.

Peggy's Tomato Tart

This tart recipe was adapted by a friend. If you love the taste of tomatoes in the summer, you will love this tart. It is also a marvelous accompaniment to grilled meats or poultry.

1 3/4 cups flour
1/2 teaspoon salt
1 tablespoon sugar
12 tablespoons cold butter, cut into pieces
1/4 cup ice water
1/3 cup Dijon mustard
1 pound mozzarella cheese, thinly sliced
6 to 8 medium tomatoes, thinly sliced
1 tablespoon chopped garlic
1/3 cup chopped black olives
1 teaspoon Herbes de Provence
Pepper to taste
2 tablespoons olive oil

Combine the flour, 1/2 teaspoon salt and sugar in a food processor container. Add the butter and process until crumbly. Add the water in a steady stream, processing constantly until the mixture forms a ball. Cover and chill for 30 minutes.

Roll the dough into a large circle 1/8 inch thick on a lightly floured surface. Fit into a 10-inch tart pan.

Brush the pastry with the Dijon mustard. Top with the cheese, covering the bottom completely. Arrange the tomatoes in 3 overlapping concentric circles over the cheese, beginning at the outer edge. Sprinkle with the garlic, olives and Herbes de Provence. Season with the pepper and additional salt. Drizzle with the olive oil.

Place the tart pan on a baking sheet. Bake at 400 degrees for 40 minutes or until cooked through.

The pastry may be frozen before baking.

The original version of this recipe calls for 1 teaspoon oregano for seasoning and no black olives or Herbes de Provence and suggests the tart can be made successfully with zucchini or eggplant.

Yields 6 to 8 servings.

Sis de Bordenave

Corn Pie

1 cup flour
1 cup yellow cornmeal
4 teaspoons baking powder
1/4 teaspoon salt
1 cup butter, softened
1 cup sugar
4 eggs
1 (4-ounce) can chopped green chiles
1 (16-ounce) can cream-style corn
1/2 cup shredded Monterey Jack cheese
1/2 cup shredded mild Cheddar cheese

Preheat the oven to 350 degrees.

Sift the flour, cornmeal, baking powder and salt together.

Cream the butter and sugar in a mixer bowl until light and fluffy. Beat in the eggs 1 at a time.

Add the green chiles, corn, Monterey Jack cheese and Cheddar cheese and mix well.

Blend in the flour mixture. Pour into a greased and floured 8x12-inch baking dish.

Reduce the oven temperature to 300 degrees. Bake for 1 hour.

Yields 10 servings.

Blueberry-Stuffed French Toast with Blueberry Sauce

12 slices white bread, cubed
12 ounces Neufchâtel cheese, cubed
1 cup blueberries, rinsed, drained
8 eggs
2 egg whites
1/3 cup maple syrup
2 cups low-fat milk
3/4 cup sugar
2 tablespoons cornstarch
1 cup water
1 cup blueberries, rinsed, drained

Arrange half the bread in a buttered 9x13-inch glass baking dish. Layer the cheese and 1 cup blueberries over the bread. Top with the remaining bread.

Whisk the eggs, egg whites, syrup and milk in a bowl. Pour over the bread mixture. Chill, covered, overnight.

Bake, covered with foil, at 350 degrees for 30 minutes. Bake, uncovered, for 30 minutes longer or until puffed and golden brown.

Combine the sugar, cornstarch and water in a small saucepan. Cook over moderately high heat for 5 minutes or until thickened, stirring occasionally. Stir in 1 cup blueberries. Simmer for 10 minutes or until the blueberries burst, stirring occasionally. Serve over the French toast.

Yields 6 servings.

Dorothy Robbins

Sausage and Cheese Loaf

This loaf can be assembled the night before; just wrap it in plastic and chill overnight.

Serve on a platter or slice and serve individually.

2 tablespoons butter
2 tablespoons flour
1 cup milk
2/3 cup shredded Swiss cheese
2 tablespoons grated Parmesan cheese
6 eggs, beaten
1/8 teaspoon nutmeg
1/8 teaspoon cayenne
8 ounces cooked sausage
1 loaf refrigerator French bread

Melt the butter in a saucepan. Stir in the flour. Add the milk gradually. Cook until the mixture boils and is thickened, stirring constantly. Remove from the heat. Add the Swiss cheese and Parmesan cheese, stirring until the cheese is melted.

Whisk the eggs, nutmeg and cayenne in a bowl. Scramble the eggs with the sausage in a skillet. Combine with the cheese mixture in a bowl and mix well.

Unroll the bread dough and spread with the cheese mixture. Roll as for a jelly roll and place on a lightly greased baking sheet.

Bake at 375 degrees for 25 minutes or until golden brown.

Yields 8 to 12 servings.

James Mahoney

Soufflé Roll with Savory Filling

1/4 cup butter
1/2 cup flour
1/2 teaspoon salt
1/8 teaspoon white pepper
2 cups milk
5 egg yolks
5 egg whites
Savory Filling

Grease a 10x15-inch baking pan. Line with waxed paper, grease again and dust with flour.

Melt the butter in a saucepan. Blend in the flour, salt and pepper. Add the milk gradually, stirring after each addition. Bring to a boil, stirring constantly. Cook for 1 minute. Beat the egg yolks slightly in a bowl. Add a small amount of the hot mixture to the egg yolks; add the egg yolks to the hot mixture. Cook over medium heat for 1 minute, stirring constantly; do not boil. Cool to room temperature, stirring occasionally.

Beat the egg whites in a mixer bowl until stiff but not dry. Fold into the cooled sauce. Spread in the prepared pan.

Bake at 400 degrees for 25 to 30 minutes or until puffed and brown. Invert onto a clean towel. Spread with the warm filling. Roll as for a jelly roll and place seam side down on a serving platter.

Yields 4 to 6 servings.

Savory Filling

2 tablespoons butter
4 shallots, finely chopped
4 medium mushrooms, chopped
1 cup chopped cooked spinach
1 cup chopped cooked ham
1 tablespoon Dijon mustard
1/4 teaspoon nutmeg
6 ounces cream cheese, softened
Salt and pepper to taste

Melt the butter in a skillet. Add the shallots. Sauté until tender. Add the mushrooms. Cook for 3 minutes or until the liquid from the mushrooms evaporates.

Add the spinach, ham, Dijon mustard, nutmeg and cream cheese. Cook until heated through, stirring frequently. Season with the salt and pepper.

Yields 2 cups.

Mary Newman

Tomato and Spinach Strata with Tomato Sauce

1 tablespoon olive oil
2 onions, chopped
4 cups sliced mushrooms
1/2 teaspoon salt
1/2 teaspoon freshly ground pepper
2 pounds nonfat cottage cheese
2 (10-ounce) packages frozen chopped spinach, thawed, squeezed dry
1/4 teaspoon nutmeg
Tomato Sauce
1 (1-pound) loaf Italian bread, cut into 1/4-inch slices
1/2 pound part skim milk mozzarella cheese, thinly sliced
4 eggs
4 egg whites
2 cups skim milk
1/3 cup freshly grated Parmesan cheese
2 tablespoons chopped fresh parsley

Heat half the olive oil in a skillet. Add the onions. Cook until softened but not brown. Remove to a bowl. Add the remaining olive oil and mushrooms to the skillet. Sauté until the liquid evaporates. Combine the mushrooms with the onions. Season with the salt and pepper.

Drain the cottage cheese in a cheesecloth-lined bowl. Combine the cottage cheese and spinach in a bowl and mix well. Season with the nutmeg and additional salt and pepper.

Spoon half the tomato sauce into a lightly oiled 8x12-inch baking dish. Layer 1/3 of the bread, half the spinach mixture, 1/3 of the bread, half the mushroom mixture, the mozzarella cheese, remaining bread, remaining spinach mixture and remaining mushroom mixture over the sauce. Top with the remaining tomato sauce.

Whisk the eggs, egg whites and skim milk in a bowl. Pierce the bread several times and pour the egg mixture over the strata. Chill, covered, overnight.

Bake at 375 degrees for 40 to 50 minutes or until heated through. Top with the Parmesan cheese. Bake for 10 minutes longer or until puffed and brown. Let stand for 10 minutes. Sprinkle with the parsley. Cut into squares.

Yields 8 servings.

Tomato Sauce

1 1/2 teaspoons olive oil
1 onion, coarsely chopped
5 cloves of garlic, minced
2 (28-ounce) cans plum tomatoes, drained
1 bay leaf
1/2 teaspoon thyme and/or oregano
2 tablespoons chopped fresh parsley
Salt and pepper to taste

Heat the olive oil in a skillet. Add the onion. Sauté for 3 to 5 minutes or until tender. Add the garlic. Sauté for 2 minutes. Add the tomatoes, bay leaf and thyme. Cook over medium heat for 15 to 20 minutes or until thickened, stirring to break up the tomatoes. Stir in the parsley, salt and pepper. Remove the bay leaf.

This may be prepared up to 2 days ahead. Cover and store in the refrigerator.

Yields 4 to 6 cups.

Glenda Tabaczynski

Hearty Open-Faced Hot Lentil Sandwiches

This is one of dozens of sandwiches that I have made for home and for our very special MIT weekly committee meetings. They have great appetites!

1/3 cup dried brown lentils
1/2 large or 1 small red bell pepper
1/4 cup sliced scallions
1 clove of garlic, minced
12 ounces fresh mushrooms, thinly sliced
1 tablespoon olive oil
1 tablespoon fresh lemon juice
1 tablespoon Worcestershire sauce
1/8 teaspoon Tabasco sauce
2 tablespoons snipped fresh basil
1 tablespoon snipped fresh thyme
Salt and freshly ground pepper to taste
1 cup grated Jarlsberg cheese
1 loaf French bread
1/2 cup minced fresh parsley

Simmer the lentils in water to cover by 2 inches for 20 minutes or just until tender. Drain in a colander, rinse with cold water and drain again. Cut the red pepper into 1/4 strips and then into 1-inch lengths.

Sauté the red pepper, scallions, garlic and mushrooms in the olive oil in a skillet until most of the liquid has evaporated. Remove from the heat. Stir in the lemon juice, Worcestershire sauce, Tabasco sauce, basil and thyme. Combine with the lentils and Jarlsberg cheese in a 3-quart bowl and mix well.

Slice the bread into halves lengthwise and scoop out the centers. Stuff each half with half the vegetable mixture. Wrap each half in foil and place on a baking sheet.

Bake at 350 degrees for 15 to 20 minutes or until heated through. Unwrap and sprinkle with the parsley. Cut each half into 4 pieces.

Serve immediately with crisp pickles and crudités.

Yields 8 servings.

Shirley R. McGowan

Curried Chicken in Puffs

1 chicken breast
3 medium carrots
1½ cups water
½ cup butter
1 cup water
1 tablespoon lemon juice
1 cup flour
1 teaspoon curry powder
5 eggs
6 mushrooms, sliced
½ cup finely chopped onion
3 ribs celery, sliced
½ cup chopped green bell pepper
½ cup chopped red bell pepper
1 tablespoon olive oil
3 tablespoons flour
3 tablespoons olive oil
½ teaspoon salt
½ teaspoon curry powder
1 tablespoon lemon juice

Boil the chicken and carrots in 1½ cups water in a saucepan until the chicken is cooked through. Reserve the broth. Chop the chicken and carrots and set aside.

For the puffs, bring the butter, 1 cup water and 1 tablespoon lemon juice to a boil in a saucepan. Add a mixture of 1 cup flour and 1 teaspoon curry powder all at once and mix well. Remove from the heat. Beat in the eggs 1 at a time. Spoon batter into 6 mounds onto a greased baking sheet. Bake at 400 degrees for 35 minutes. Cool slightly and cut ⅓ off the tops.

For the filling, sauté the mushrooms, onion, celery, green pepper and red pepper in 1 tablespoon olive oil in a skillet. Remove the vegetables with a slotted spoon and set aside. Stir 3 tablespoons flour and 3 tablespoons oil into the skillet.

Add the reserved broth, chicken, carrots, mushroom mixture, salt, ½ teaspoon curry powder and 1 tablespoon lemon juice. Cook until thickened, stirring constantly. Spoon into the puffs and replace the tops.

Serve with mandarin orange segments over lettuce leaves.

Yields 6 servings.

Grace R. W. Hall

Hot Chicken Salad

6 cups chopped cooked chicken breast
4 cups chopped celery
1 cup sliced almonds
1 (2-ounce) can pimento, drained (optional)
2½ cups mayonnaise
6 tablespoons lemon juice
2 tablespoons grated onion
2 teaspoons salt
1 teaspoon pepper
2 cups crushed potato chips
1 cup shredded Cheddar cheese

Combine the chicken, celery, almonds, pimento, mayonnaise, lemon juice, onion, salt and pepper in a bowl and mix well. Spoon into a lightly greased 3-quart casserole. Cover with a mixture of the potato chips and cheese.

Bake, covered, at 375 degrees for 30 minutes. Bake, uncovered, for 15 minutes.

Yields 8 to 12 servings.

Rebecca M. Vest

Oriental Chicken Salad

3 whole chicken breasts, boned
36 pea pods
1 package Near East rice pilaf, cooked
3 ribs celery, sliced diagonally
1 bunch scallions, chopped
3 slices fresh gingerroot, peeled, finely chopped
1 package frozen tiny peas, thawed, rinsed
1 small can water chestnuts, sliced
1 yellow bell pepper, julienned
1 red bell pepper, julienned
1 cup unsalted cashews or toasted sliced almonds
1/4 cup sesame oil
1 tablespoon rice wine vinegar
2 tablespoons soy sauce
2 tablespoons Dijon mustard
1/2 cup Italian salad dressing
1/2 cup mayonnaise
Boston lettuce

Poach the chicken; let cool to room temperature and chop. Steam the pea pods for 2 minutes. Cut them into halves.

Combine the chicken, pea pods, rice pilaf, celery, scallions, gingerroot, peas, water chestnuts, yellow pepper, red pepper and cashews in a large bowl and toss to mix.

Combine the sesame oil, vinegar, soy sauce, Dijon mustard, salad dressing and mayonnaise in a bowl and whisk until smooth. Toss with the chicken mixture. Serve on a bed of Boston lettuce leaves.

You may add steamed asparagus tips, chopped artichoke hearts, sliced radishes or other favorite vegetables to the chicken mixture.

Yields 8 servings.

Marie Salah

Kedgeree

1 1/2 pounds smoked haddock (finnan haddie)
2 cups water
1/4 cup butter
1 medium onion, chopped
3/4 teaspoon hot curry powder
1 cup long grain white rice
2 cups water
3 hard-cooked eggs, peeled, chopped
3 tablespoons chopped parsley
1 tablespoon lemon juice
1/4 cup butter

Combine the haddock and 2 cups water in a large skillet. Bring to a boil. Simmer gently, covered, for 8 minutes; drain. Remove the haddock to a dish and cover with foil to keep warm.

Melt 1/4 cup butter in a saucepan. Add the onion. Cook for 5 minutes or until tender but not brown. Stir in the curry powder. Cook for 1 minute. Stir in the rice and 2 cups water. Simmer, tightly covered, for 15 minutes or until the rice is tender.

Remove and discard the skin from the fish. Flake the fish. Add the fish, eggs, parsley, lemon juice and 1/4 cup butter to the rice mixture. Cover the saucepan with a folded tea towel. Cook over very low heat for 5 minutes.

Pour into a hot serving dish and season to taste.

Yields 4 servings.

Dorothy Robbins

Primordial Chemistry

(Soups & Salads)

MIT
Women's League

Classical Soup Making

One of my most favorite things to do in the kitchen is making a pot of soup. I have found an easy way which has revolutionized soup making for me. Since I often have chicken broth from poaching chicken, I freeze it and save it for soups.

To make the broth, cover 5 pounds of chicken with water in a large pot. Add 2 teaspoons salt, a few peppercorns, 2 bay leaves, 2 teaspoons thyme, 3 sliced ribs of celery, 1 peeled and sliced onion, 1 peeled and sliced carrot and white wine. Bring to a boil and simmer until the chicken is tender. Remove and discard the bay leaves. The chicken makes a heavenly chicken salad, and the broth makes a wonderful soup stock. You can make beautiful soups by using broccoli, asparagus, zucchini, cauliflower, ginger or curried carrot, carrot and parsnip, or other vegetables.

Melt 2 tablespoons butter or margarine in a large pot. Add 1/2 cup chopped onion and sauté until tender. Add 3 cups sliced vegetables of your choice, 3/4 cup chopped peeled potato, 1/2 cup sliced celery and 4 cups chicken broth. Cover and bring to a boil. Reduce the heat and simmer until the vegetables are very tender. Purée in small batches in a blender or food processor. (To my great joy, I found a wonderful gadget which purées right in the pot—Household Blender Mixer by Braun.) Add salt, pepper and other seasonings to taste. Heat gently before serving. Remember, many soups, such as zucchini or asparagus, are wonderful served cold, especially for summertime luncheons.

After the soup has been blended, there are many things you may add to make a glorious soup.

For asparagus soup—a bit of cream; grated sharp cheese; lovage or tarragon

For broccoli soup—sharp cheese or Gorgonzola cheese

For zucchini soup—basil or a bit of marjoram

For tomato soup—basil or a bit of marjoram

For carrot soup—curry, dill or fresh ginger

For mushroom soup—cream; thyme or basil

For cauliflower soup—basil, rosemary or tarragon

If needed, thin the soup a bit by adding more chicken broth or white wine.

Have a great time making your own variations.

Yield is variable.

Martha H. Harleman

Off with the Fat

If there is a thick layer of fat on the surface of hot soup, drop in 4 or 5 ice cubes. Fish them out immediately with a slotted spoon. Repeat if necessary.

Russian Cabbage and Beef Soup

This is an adaptation of a recipe for S'Chee (Russian Cabbage Soup) that replaced the long process of homemade stock with canned stock and adds some additional ingredients. When I brought some to work, three people said it was absolutely the most delicious soup they had ever tasted–and wanted the recipe (I think the secret is the sauerkraut). It makes a lot, but even with only 2 of us in the house, we use it up easily.

5 sprigs of parsley
2 celery tops
2 bay leaves
5 slices bacon, chopped
3 pounds boneless chuck, cut into 1/2-inch cubes
2 tablespoons vegetable oil
4 medium onions, finely chopped
3 cloves of garlic, minced
1 1/2 teaspoons caraway seeds
1/3 cup flour
1/4 cup red wine vinegar
1 1/2 tablespoons tomato paste
5 cups canned beef broth
5 cups water
1 (28-ounce) can solid pack tomatoes, drained, chopped
1/2 teaspoon salt
1/4 cup vegetable oil
1 cup finely chopped onion
1/2 cup each finely chopped celery and carrot
1 teaspoon chopped garlic
1 pound fresh or canned sauerkraut, rinsed, chopped
7 cups shredded cabbage
1/4 cup sugar
3 tablespoons lemon juice
2 cups sour cream (optional)
1/4 cup chopped fresh dill (optional)

Tie the parsley sprigs, celery tops and bay leaves in a cheesecloth bag to make an herb bouquet.

Cook the bacon in a heavy 8-quart kettle over moderate heat until crisp. Remove to a large bowl with a slotted spoon. Add the chuck to the bacon drippings in the kettle in small batches. Cook until browned. Remove to the bowl with a slotted spoon.

Reduce the heat to moderate and add 2 tablespoons oil. Add 4 onions and 3 garlic cloves. Cook until golden brown. Stir in the caraway seeds and flour. Cook for 2 minutes, stirring constantly. Whisk in the vinegar and tomato paste. Cook for 1 minute, whisking constantly; the mixture will be very thick. Add the beef broth, water, herb bouquet, tomatoes, bacon, chuck and salt. Bring to a boil. Simmer very gently for 2 hours, stirring occasionally.

Heat 1/4 cup oil in a large heavy skillet. Add 1 cup onion, 1/2 cup celery, carrot and 1 teaspoon garlic. Cook over low heat for 15 minutes or just until the vegetables color, stirring occasionally. Add the sauerkraut. Cook briskly for 1 to 2 minutes. Reduce the heat and stir in the cabbage. Cook over moderate heat until the cabbage begins to wilt, stirring frequently. Reduce the heat and partially cover the skillet. Add 1 spoonful of stock from the kettle every 8 minutes to moisten the vegetables. Let braise for 30 minutes and set aside.

Remove the herb bouquet from the soup. Add the braised vegetables, sugar and lemon juice. Bring to a boil. Simmer gently, partially covered, for 1 1/2 hours.

Serve in large bowls. Add a dollop of sour cream to each bowl and sprinkle with dill.

Yields 12 servings.

Betsy Millard

New England Clam Chowder

This recipe has been used by the Women's League Adventures in Eating Group for their annual clambake for 20 years and has been enjoyed by all. Pilot crackers are the traditional accompaniment.

4 ounces bacon, cut into 1/8-inch cubes
1 cup finely chopped onion
3 cups cold water
4 cups potatoes, cut into 1/4-inch cubes
2 cups fresh minced clams with juices, or 2 (8-ounce) cans chopped clams
2 cups whipping cream
1/3 teaspoon thyme
Salt and freshly ground pepper to taste
2 tablespoons butter, softened
Paprika to taste

Fry the bacon in a heavy saucepan over high heat for 3 minutes or until a thin film of fat covers the pan, stirring constantly. Reduce the heat to moderate. Add the onion. Cook for 5 minutes or until light golden brown, stirring occasionally. Add the water and potatoes. Bring to a boil over high heat; reduce the heat. Simmer, partially covered, for 15 minutes or until the potatoes are tender but not mushy.

Add the undrained clams, whipping cream and thyme. Bring almost to a boil. Season with the salt and pepper. Stir in the butter and sprinkle with the paprika.

If you double or triple this recipe, adjust the cooking time accordingly.

Yields 6 to 8 servings.

Elizabeth E. Kleiman

Cold Cucumber Soup

3 cups chopped peeled cucumbers
1 cup chopped walnuts
1/4 cup chopped fresh dill
2 teaspoons salt
1/2 teaspoon pepper
2 cloves of garlic, minced
1/4 cup olive oil
2 cups sour cream or yogurt

Combine the cucumbers, walnuts, dill, salt, pepper, garlic and olive oil in a bowl and mix well. Marinate in the refrigerator overnight.

Add the sour cream at serving time; the mixture will be thick. Place 1 ice cube in each soup bowl. Pour in the soup.

Yields 4 to 6 servings.

Maureen Feldman

Making Parmesan Curls

Shave a large piece of room-temperature Parmesan cheese into curls with a sharp vegetable peeler. To avoid breaking the curls, add them to salads after the salads are tossed.

Cold Eggplant Parsley Soup

1 (1-pound) eggplant, peeled, cubed
2 teaspoons salt
1 onion, minced
1 tablespoon olive oil
2 cloves of garlic, minced
1 teaspoon curry powder
4$^1/_2$ cups canned chicken broth
Salt and pepper to taste
$^1/_4$ cup minced fresh parsley
Fresh lemon juice to taste

Toss the eggplant with the salt in a colander. Let drain for 20 minutes. Rinse under cold running water and drain well.

Combine the onion and olive oil in a heavy aucepan. Cook over moderately low heat for 3 minutes or until the onion is tender, stirring occasionally. Add the garlic. Cook for 1 minute, stirring constantly. Add the curry powder. Cook for 1 minute, stirring constantly. Add the chicken broth. Bring to a boil. Add the eggplant. Simmer, covered, for 40 minutes. Purée the soup in batches in a blender or food processor fitted with a steel blade. Remove to a bowl. Season with the salt and pepper to taste. Let cool. Chill, covered, for 2 hours to overnight.

Stir in the parsley and lemon juice. Ladle into chilled soup bowls.

Yields 4 servings.

Lee C. Bradley

Harvest Soup

8 ounces mild Italian sausage, cut into small pieces
$^1/_2$ cup chopped green bell pepper
$^1/_2$ cup chopped onion
1 cup sliced zucchini
1 clove of garlic, minced
2 tablespoons chopped parsley
$^1/_2$ teaspoon oregano
2 (14-ounce) cans chicken broth
1 (14-ounce) can stewed tomatoes, chopped
6 ounces tortellini
Salt and pepper to taste
Grated Parmesan cheese to taste

Brown the sausage in a large pot and drain most of the fat. Add the green pepper and onion. Sauté until tender. Add the zucchini, garlic, parsley and oregano. Cook until the zucchini is tender. Add the chicken broth and tomatoes. Bring to a boil. Add the tortellini and reduce the heat. Simmer for 35 to 40 minutes or until heated through. Season with the salt and pepper.

Ladle into bowls. Sprinkle with the cheese.

Yields 4 to 5 servings.

Marilyn A. MacLellan

Lentil Soup

I got this recipe from Mel Binder, an alto saxophone player in the Middlesex Concert Band, where I play piccolo.

2 carrots, chopped
1 green bell pepper, chopped
1 medium onion, chopped
1 rib celery, chopped
Vegetable oil
1 (16-ounce) can tomato sauce
1/2 jigger cooking sherry
2 drops of Tabasco sauce
1 cup dried lentils
3 cups water
1 teaspoon salt, or to taste
1/4 tablespoon pepper, or to taste

Sauté the carrots, green pepper, onion and celery in the oil in a skillet.

Combine the sautéed vegetables, tomato sauce, sherry, Tabasco sauce, lentils, water, salt and pepper in a 3-quart pot. Bring to a boil. Simmer, covered, until the vegetables are tender, adding additional water if needed.

Yields 4 to 6 servings.

Michael Bleiweiss

Cream of Mushroom Soup

12 ounces mushrooms, finely chopped
6 tablespoons butter
10 tablespoons flour
4 cups hot rich chicken stock
2 cups half-and-half
1/2 cup ground walnuts
Dark rum (optional)
Fresh parsley

Sauté the mushrooms in a nonstick skillet. Melt the butter in a large pot. Add the flour. Cook for 2 minutes, stirring constantly. Add the chicken stock. Cook until thickened and boiling, stirring constantly.

Add the half-and-half, mushrooms and walnuts. Cook until heated through.

Ladle into bowls. When serving, add a splash of rum to each bowl and garnish with parsley.

Yields 6 servings.

Thickening Soups or Sauces

Instant dehydrated mashed potato flakes added to your homemade vegetable soup will act as both a thickener and a flavor enhancer.

Prince Michael of Kent Soup

As served to His Royal Highness when visiting Newport, Rhode Island

2 (46-ounce) cans chicken stock
2 (46-ounce) cans vegetable juice cocktail or tomato juice
4 carrots, finely chopped
6 ribs celery, finely chopped
1 large onion, finely chopped
5 cloves of garlic, finely chopped
6 egg whites
Bouquet garni (bay leaf, basil, salt, pepper, parsley stems)
Tabasco sauce and salt to taste
Sherry to taste

Combine the chicken stock and vegetable juice in a large heavy pot. Add the carrots, celery, onion, garlic, egg whites and bouquet garni. Bring to a boil over high heat, stirring until the vegetables appear to be suspended. Reduce the heat and simmer until a raft (cooked vegetables floating at the top of the pot) has formed; do not boil. Strain off the raft through a cheesecloth-lined colander. Stir in the Tabasco sauce, salt and sherry. Garnish with mushrooms, lobster or shrimp.

Yields 8 to 12 servings.

Peter Rhein

Pumpkin Soup

1 large onion, minced
3 tablespoons butter or margarine
3 tablespoons flour
2 cups milk
2 cups chicken stock
1 3/4 cups fresh or canned cooked pumpkin or butternut squash
2 teaspoons sugar
1/2 teaspoon freshly ground nutmeg
2 teaspoons salt
1/4 teaspoon white pepper
1/2 cup whipping cream, milk or half-and-half, heated
3 tablespoons sherry

Sauté the onion in the butter in a 3-quart saucepan. Stir in the flour. Cook for 1 minute. Add 2 cups milk and the chicken stock. Cook until slightly thickened, stirring occasionally. Add the pumpkin. Stir in the sugar, nutmeg, salt and pepper. Bring to a boil. Adjust the seasonings. Stir in the whipping cream and sherry.

Pour into a warm soup tureen.

Yields 4 to 6 servings.

Muriel Petranic

Zucchini Soup

3 cups chopped zucchini
2 cups heated chicken bouillon
1/4 teaspoon curry
1/2 teaspoon dill
Salt and pepper to taste
8 ounces cream cheese, softened

Cook the zucchini in the chicken bouillon in a large pot until tender. Season with the curry, dill, salt and pepper.

Combine with the cream cheese in a blender or food processor container. Purée until smooth.

This is best served chilled, but it may be served warm.

Yields 4 to 6 servings.

Rebecca M. Vest

Avocado Magic

Don't worry if your avocado is not ripe for that special dinner party. Just bury your avocados in a canister of all-purpose flour for 24 hours and they will emerge soft and ready to use.

Bean Salad

1 can black beans
1 can black-eyed peas
1 can green peas
1 can red kidney beans
1 can fava beans
1 can white kidney beans
1 can chickpeas
1 teaspoon salt, or to taste
1/2 teaspoon pepper, or to taste
3 tablespoons extra-virgin olive oil
6 to 8 tablespoons finely chopped fresh cilantro
1 to 2 cloves of fresh garlic, crushed (optional)

Rinse the beans and peas thoroughly in a colander.

Combine with the salt, pepper, olive oil, cilantro and garlic in a large bowl and mix well. Chill overnight.

Yields 15 to 18 servings.

Bob Weinberg

Broccoli Salad

1 bunch broccoli
10 slices bacon, crisp-fried, crumbled
1/2 cup raisins
1/4 cup chopped red onion
1/2 cup sunflower seeds
1/4 cup sugar
1/2 cup mayonnaise
2 tablespoons vinegar

Peel the stems and slice the broccoli thinly. Mix with the bacon, raisins, onion and sunflower seeds in a large bowl.

Mix the sugar, mayonnaise and vinegar in a small bowl. Add to the salad and toss to mix.

Yields 6 servings.

Peggy Heywood

Lemon Slices

Spread fresh lemon slices on a tray and freeze. Transfer the frozen slices to a freezer bag. Thaw at room temperature for 1 hour before using.

Brie Salad with Pecans, Celery and Orange Vinaigrette

Kit is the daughter of James R. Killian, Jr., past president of MIT.

1/2 cup vegetable oil
1/2 cup walnut oil
1/3 cup balsamic vinegar
Grated zest of 1 orange
1 tablespoon minced garlic
Freshly ground pepper to taste
1 green apple, cut into 12 thin slices
1 red apple, cut into 12 thin slices
2 large heads Boston lettuce, thinly sliced
1 large red onion, thinly sliced
1 cup chopped celery
1 pound Brie cheese, cut into 12 slices
3/4 cup toasted chopped pecans

For the vinaigrette, mix the vegetable oil, walnut oil, vinegar, orange zest, garlic and pepper in a medium bowl. Coat the apple slices with a small amount of the vinaigrette in a bowl. Toss the lettuce and onions with the remaining vinaigrette in a bowl.

Arrange the lettuce and onions on salad plates. Arrange the apple slices and celery over the lettuce and onions. Top with the cheese. Sprinkle with the pecans.

Yields 12 servings.

Carolyn Killian Staley

Carolina Coleslaw

1 large head cabbage, chopped
1 medium green bell pepper, chopped
1 medium red onion, chopped
1 cup sugar
1 teaspoon salt
1 teaspoon dry mustard
1 teaspoon celery seed
1 cup cider vinegar
2/3 cup vegetable oil

Mix the cabbage, green pepper and onion in a large bowl.

Combine the sugar, salt, dry mustard and celery seed in a saucepan. Add the vinegar and oil. Bring to a boil, stirring until the sugar is dissolved. Pour the hot dressing over the cabbage mixture and toss well. Cool to room temperature. Chill until serving time.

Yields 10 to 12 servings.

Rebecca M. Vest

Caesar Salad

John Deutch, currently CIA Director, is a past, present and future MIT-er. He is on leave from his position of Institute Professor.

1 teaspoon salt
1/2 teaspoon freshly ground pepper
3 large cloves of garlic, minced
1 teaspoon Dijon mustard
1 teaspoon Worcestershire sauce
2 tablespoons chicken broth
2 tablespoons olive oil
1/2 cup fresh lemon juice
1/4 cup grated imported Parmesan cheese
2 large heads romaine lettuce
1 small can anchovies (optional)
Croutons (optional)

Combine the salt, pepper, garlic, Dijon mustard, Worcestershire sauce, chicken broth and olive oil in a blender container. Add the lemon juice and cheese. Pulse several times until well mixed; the dressing will be thick. Cover and chill until serving time.

Tear the lettuce into bite-sized pieces into a large bowl. Toss with the dressing. Top with the anchovies and croutons.

Yields 4 to 6 servings.

Pat and John Deutch

Carrot Salad

1 1/2 pounds carrots, thinly sliced, blanched
1 medium onion, thinly sliced
1/2 cup vegetable oil
1/2 cup sugar
1/2 cup cider vinegar
1 teaspoon celery seed
1/4 teaspoon dry mustard
1/4 teaspoon salt

Mix the carrots and onion in a large bowl.

Combine the oil, sugar, vinegar, celery seed, dry mustard and salt in a medium bowl and mix well. Pour over the carrot mixture. Marinate in the refrigerator for several hours to overnight. Drain before serving.

Yields 4 to 6 servings.

Rebecca M. Vest

Cranberry Wine Salad

1 (6-ounce) package raspberry gelatin
2 cups boiling water
1 (16-ounce) can whole cranberry sauce
1 (8-ounce) can unsweetened crushed pineapple
1/2 cup port
1/4 cup chopped walnuts

Dissolve the gelatin in the boiling water. Stir in the cranberry sauce, undrained pineapple and port. Chill until partially set. Fold in the walnuts.

Pour into a 1 1/2-quart mold. Chill until set.

Yields 6 to 8 servings.

Janice Kispert

Chick-Chick Salad

This is a wonderful way to use up leftover chicken and is very popular at my house. I think I invented it myself, but then who knows. The curry dressing is fairly common in Switzerland for exotic salads.

1 cup chopped cooked chicken or turkey
1 can chickpeas, drained
3 ribs celery, chopped
1 red or green bell pepper, chopped
1/2 zucchini, finely chopped
2 tablespoons mayonnaise
2 tablespoons plain low-fat yogurt
1 teaspoon curry powder, or to taste
Salt and pepper to taste
1 teaspoon lemon juice
1 teaspoon mustard

Mix the chicken, chickpeas, celery, red pepper and zucchini in a large bowl.

Mix the mayonnaise, yogurt, curry powder, salt, pepper, lemon juice and mustard in a medium bowl. Toss with the salad. Garnish with black olives and/or parsley.

Yields 2 to 3 servings.

Sylvia Einstein

Corn Salad

6 ears of corn, steamed or boiled
2 tablespoons mayonnaise
1/4 teaspoon salt
1/4 teaspoon pepper
Juice of 1/2 lemon

Cut the corn kernels from the cobs with a sharp knife.

Combine the corn, mayonnaise, salt, pepper and lemon juice in a bowl and mix well.

Yields 4 to 6 servings.

Bob Weinberg

Making Your Own Curry Powder

Combine 3 tablespoons coriander seeds, 2 tablespoons cumin seeds, 2 tablespoons turmeric, 1 tablespoon mustard seeds, the seeds of 8 cardamom pods, 8 cloves, 1 1/2 teaspoons ground ginger, 1 1/2 teaspoons freshly grated nutmeg, and 1/4 teaspoon cayenne in a jelly roll pan. Toast in a 250-degree oven for 20 minutes. Let cool to room temperature. Pulverize in an electric spice grinder or coffee grinder and strain through a sieve into a bowl. The curry powder will keep in a tightly sealed jar in a cool dark place for up to 6 months.
Yields approximately 1/2 cup.

Indian Summer Salad

Dave Danells is currently the Associate Food Service Director at Walker. Prior to this, he was the Executive Chef for MIT Catering, Lobdell Food Court and Networks Restaurant. He has been with Aramark at MIT for 6 years.

1 large red onion, sliced
1/3 cup red wine vinegar
1/2 cup water
2 teaspoons honey
1/4 teaspoon kosher salt
5 peppercorns, crushed
1 teaspoon oregano
1 teaspoon basil leaves
12 new potatoes, steamed
12 small yellow beets, steamed
8 ounces green beans, steamed
3 cups vinaigrette
1 head romaine lettuce, rinsed
1 red bell pepper, julienned
1 green bell pepper, julienned
18 cherry tomatoes, cut into halves
8 hard-cooked eggs, peeled, cut into halves
24 olives
2 tablespoons capers

Bring the onion, vinegar, water, honey, salt, pepper, oregano and basil to a boil in a saucepan. Simmer for 8 minutes. Cool to room temperature. Chill for 2 hours or longer.

Place the potatoes, beets and beans in separate bowls. Divide the vinaigrette between them and toss.

Arrange the lettuce on a serving platter. Place the potatoes in the center. Surround the potatoes with the beans, peppers, tomatoes, eggs, beets and pickled onion. Top with the olives and capers. Drizzle with the vinaigrette as needed.

Yields 8 servings.

Dave Danells

Orzo Salad

2 cups orzo
1 cup crumbled feta cheese
2/3 cup minced fresh parsley
2/3 cup minced fresh basil or dill
3 tomatoes, chopped
1/4 cup lemon juice
1/3 cup olive oil
Salt and pepper to taste

Cook the orzo using the package directions until al dente. Drain and rinse with cold water. Combine with the cheese, parsley, basil and tomatoes in a large bowl.

Mix the lemon juice, olive oil, salt and pepper in a small bowl. Pour over the salad and toss.

Serve chilled.

Yields 8 servings.

Dad's Roasted Red Pepper Salad

This was a winter salad in our home. My mother roasted and canned red peppers in the fall, and my father enjoyed making the salad. It was eaten with freshly delivered Italian bread. It can be mixed with salad greens or served as an appetizer or side dish.

6 to 8 red bell peppers
3 cloves of garlic, crushed
1 teaspoon oregano, or to taste
1/4 cup olive oil
Salt and pepper to taste

Roast the peppers at 400 degrees for 40 to 50 minutes or until the skin is blistered and the peppers are soft enough to peel. Peel the peppers, remove the seeds and stem and cut into 1-inch slices.

Mix with the garlic, oregano, olive oil, salt and pepper in a bowl. Chill for 1 to 2 days to allow the flavors to blend. Bring to room temperature before serving.

You may substitute three 7-ounce jars of roasted red peppers (without vinegar) for the fresh peppers.

Yields 6 to 8 servings.

Joanne M. Orlando

Potato Salad with Dill

5 medium red potatoes
1/2 cup sour cream
1/2 cup mayonnaise
2 green onions, thinly sliced
1 tablespoon minced fresh dill
2 teaspoons Dijon mustard
1 1/2 teaspoons lemon juice
1/2 teaspoon salt
Freshly ground pepper to taste

Place the potatoes in water to cover in a saucepan. Bring to a boil. Cook over medium heat for 30 minutes or until tender. Rinse with cold water and let cool. Cut into 1/2-inch pieces and remove to a large bowl.

Mix the sour cream, mayonnaise, green onions, dill, Dijon mustard, lemon juice, salt and pepper in a small bowl. Combine with the potatoes and mix well.

Chill, covered, overnight.

Yields 6 to 8 servings.

Sis de Bordenave

Spinach Salad with Vermouth Dressing

The secret of this salad is the dressing.

Betty is the wife of Howard W. Johnson, a past president of MIT.

1/4 cup lemon juice
1/4 cup dry vermouth
2 teaspoons dry mustard
2 teaspoons salt
1 teaspoon pepper
1 clove of garlic, pressed
3/4 cup olive oil
3/4 cup salad oil
1 1/2 pounds spinach
4 green onions, chopped
2 teaspoons crushed tarragon
4 hard-cooked eggs, peeled, sliced
6 slices bacon, crisp-fried, crumbled
2 tablespoons capers, drained
10 mushrooms, sliced

Mix the lemon juice, vermouth, dry mustard, salt, pepper, garlic, olive oil and salad oil in a covered container and shake well.

Rinse the spinach and tear into bite-size pieces. Wrap in a towel and crisp in the freezer for 5 minutes. Toss with the green onions and tarragon in a salad bowl. Chill until serving time. Add the eggs, bacon, capers and mushrooms. Toss with the dressing.

Yields 8 to 10 servings.

Betty Johnson

Potato Salad Dressing

This is Pennsylvania Dutch and has been handed down in my family from generation to generation.

1 egg
3 tablespoons sugar
1 tablespoon flour
1/4 cup vinegar
1/2 cup water
Salt to taste
1 tablespoon melted butter or bacon drippings

Beat the egg in a bowl. Stir in the sugar and flour. Add the vinegar, water and salt and mix well. Stir in the butter.

Combine with hard-cooked eggs, onion, celery, potatoes and parsley for potato salad, serve hot over endives or dandelion greens, or serve warm or cold over lettuce.

Yields 1 cup.

Carolyn Latanision

Snow Pea Salad with Sweet-and-Sour Dressing

This beautiful salad with bright crisp colors is especially nice for summer picnics, but it's much too good (and easy to prepare) to eat during only one season.

1 large yellow, red, orange or purple bell pepper
8 ounces fresh snow peas
8 ounces mushrooms, thinly sliced
Sweet-and-Sour Dressing
2 tablespoons toasted sesame seeds

Core and seed the pepper. Remove the ribs and slice thinly. Trim the snow peas and remove the strings. Blanch the peas in boiling salted water in a large pot for 1 minute. Drain and refresh under cold running water. Pat dry with paper towels.

Combine the snow peas, pepper and mushrooms in a salad bowl. Toss with enough dressing to coat. Sprinkle with the sesame seeds.

Yields 6 servings.

Sweet-and-Sour Dressing

1 to 2 teaspoons sesame oil
3 tablespoons white wine vinegar
2 tablespoons sugar
1/2 teaspoon salt
1 teaspoon freshly ground pepper
1/4 cup (or less) canola oil

Combine the sesame oil, vinegar, sugar, salt, pepper and canola oil in a covered jar and shake vigorously.

Yields 1/2 cup.

Nancy Kelly

Strawberry-Spinach Salad

2 bunches fresh spinach
1 quart fresh strawberries
1/2 teaspoon minced onion
1/4 cup cider vinegar
1/4 cup vegetable oil
1/4 cup honey
1/4 teaspoon Worcestershire sauce
2 tablespoons toasted sesame seeds
1 teaspoon poppy seeds

Rinse the spinach and tear into bite-size pieces. Drain on paper towels. Hull and rinse the strawberries. Cut the larger berries into halves. Drain on paper towels.

Combine the onion, vinegar, oil, honey and Worcestershire sauce in a blender container. Process until smooth. Stir in the sesame seeds and poppy seeds.

Combine the spinach and strawberries in a large salad bowl. Toss with the dressing and serve immediately.

This dressing will keep well in the refrigerator, but the salad will not.

Yields 10 servings.

Fruited Tuna Salad

I worked on this recipe for about three years before I was satisfied. I even tried a hot version that was so bad it was inedible.

3/4 cup mayonnaise
Juice of 1 lime
1 teaspoon curry powder, or to taste
1 1/2 cups small shell macaroni
2 ribs celery, thinly sliced
1 tablespoon chopped red onion, or to taste
1 can chunk light tuna
1 (8-ounce) can pineapple bits or chunks, drained, cut into halves
1 (3-ounce) jar capers, drained
1 (8-ounce) can mandarin oranges, drained
Fresh lettuce leaves

Mix the mayonnaise, lime juice and curry powder in a small bowl. Cook the macaroni using the package directions. Drain and cool with cold water.

Mix the macaroni, celery, onion, tuna, pineapple and capers in a large bowl. Stir in the mayonnaise mixture and the oranges. Chill until serving time.

Serve over the lettuce.

This keeps well in the refrigerator for several days.

Yields 4 servings.

Joanne Miller

Chinese Chicken Salad

3 to 4 chicken breasts, cooked, finely chopped
3 scallions, chopped
1/4 cup vinegar
1/4 cup sugar
2 teaspoons salt
1 tablespoon MSG
1/2 teaspoon pepper
1/2 cup vegetable oil
1 tablespoon poppy seeds
1/2 can sliced water chestnuts
1/4 cup lightly toasted sesame seeds
1 head lettuce, torn into small pieces
1 small can Chinese noodles
1 package slivered almonds

Mix the chicken and scallions in a large bowl and set aside.

Combine the vinegar, sugar, salt, MSG, pepper and oil in a medium bowl and mix well. Stir in the poppy seeds, water chestnuts and sesame seeds.

Add the vinegar mixture and lettuce to the chicken mixture and mix well. Top with the noodles and almonds.

Yields 4 to 6 servings.

Chutney Dressing

1/4 cup chutney
1/2 teaspoon dried hot red pepper flakes
2 tablespoons fresh lemon juice
1/3 cup water
2 large cloves of garlic, chopped
Salt to taste
1/2 cup vegetable oil

Combine the chutney, pepper flakes, lemon juice, water, garlic and salt in a blender container. Process until smooth. Add the oil in a stream with the blender running, processing until emulsified.

Yields 1 cup.

Kathleen's Curry Dressing

This recipe was given to me by Kathleen Levitt, whose husband, Raymond, was a professor of Civil Engineering. It has been used by me and many others for at least ten or twelve years with much success.

2 tablespoons white wine vinegar
1 tablespoon vermouth
1 teaspoon soy sauce
2 teaspoons Dijon mustard
1/2 teaspoon each sugar and curry powder
1/2 teaspoon salt, or to taste
1/4 teaspoon pepper
1/3 cup salad oil

Combine the vinegar, vermouth, soy sauce, Dijon mustard, sugar, curry powder, salt, pepper and oil in a small covered jar. Shake well before using.

Yields 1/2 to 3/4 cup.

Chesley T. Logcher

Jimmy's Vinny(grette)

This salad dressing is used in the MIT Alice Young Maclaurin Dining Room as the house dressing and marinade for chicken and fish. It is one of President Vest's favorites.

1/2 cup chopped Bermuda onion
3 cloves of garlic, minced
3 cups canola oil
1 cup red wine vinegar
1 tablespoon Dijon mustard
Juice of 1/2 lemon
Salt and pepper to taste
Tabasco sauce to taste

Combine the onion, garlic, oil, vinegar, Dijon mustard, lemon juice, salt, pepper and Tabasco sauce in a blender container. Process at high speed until thick and creamy.

This will keep in the refrigerator for at least a month.

Yields 4 cups.

James Mahoney

Balsamic Vinaigrette

2 tablespoons balsamic vinegar
2 tablespoons white wine vinegar
2 teaspoons Dijon mustard
1 shallot, minced
Salt and pepper to taste
2/3 cup olive oil

Whisk the vinegar, Dijon mustard, shallot, salt and pepper in a bowl. Add the oil in a stream, whisking constantly until emulsified.

Yields 1 cup.

Main Menu

(ENTRÉES)

MIT
Women's League

English Brown Stew

Always a Kleiman family favorite, served with a green salad and dunking bread!

2 pounds stewing beef
Flour
Shortening or vegetable oil, heated
5 cups boiling water
1/4 cup chopped onion
1 tablespoon salt
3/4 teaspoon pepper
3/4 teaspoon paprika
1/4 teaspoon allspice, or to taste
1 tablespoon lemon juice
1 teaspoon Worcestershire sauce
1 (8-ounce) can tomato sauce
2 teaspoons sugar
2 cups chopped onion
1 cup sliced carrots
2 cups chopped potatoes
1 cup chopped celery

Dredge the beef in the flour. Brown in the hot shortening or oil in a large pot. Add the water, 1/4 cup onion, salt, pepper, paprika, allspice, lemon juice, Worcestershire sauce, tomato sauce and sugar. Simmer, tightly covered, for 2 hours, adding additional water if needed.

Add 2 cups onion, carrots, potatoes and celery. Cook for 30 minutes longer or until the vegetables are tender.

Yields 4 to 6 servings.

Elizabeth E. Kleiman

Beef Stroganoff

1 1/2 pounds beef sirloin or round steak
3 tablespoons flour
1 teaspoon salt
1/4 teaspoon pepper
2 tablespoons butter or margarine
1 medium onion, very thinly sliced
1 pint mushrooms, sliced
2 tablespoons butter or margarine
1 tablespoon flour
1 can beef stock
1 teaspoon Dijon mustard
3/4 to 1 1/2 cups sour cream

Cut the beef into 1/2x2-inch strips. Mix 3 tablespoons flour, salt and pepper together. Dredge the beef in the flour mixture.

Sauté the beef in 2 tablespoons butter in a large saucepan. Remove the beef to a plate. Scrape the pan and reserve the browned bits. Sauté the onion and mushrooms in the pan until the onion is translucent. Add 2 tablespoons butter, 1 tablespoon flour and the pan scrapings. Stir in the beef stock gradually. Cook until thickened and smooth, stirring constantly. Add the beef. Cook, covered, over very low heat for 1 to 1 1/2 hours or until the beef is tender. Stir in the Dijon mustard and sour cream at serving time.

Serve with noodles, rice or parslied potatoes.

You may prepare this dish except for the mustard and sour cream up to 24 hours ahead. Bake at 225 to 250 degrees for 45 minutes. Let cool and refrigerate until needed. Heat through in a 250- to 275-degree oven, adding the mustard and sour cream at serving time.

Yields 4 to 6 servings.

Lillian J. Alberty

Spanish Stew

2 pounds stewing beef, trimmed, cut into 1/2-inch cubes
2 (8-ounce) cans tomato sauce
1/2 cup dry red wine
2 large onions, coarsely chopped
2 cloves of garlic, crushed
1 bay leaf
3/4 teaspoon dried thyme
2 teaspoons salt
1/2 teaspoon freshly ground pepper
12 ounces large mushrooms, cut into quarters
1 pound fettuccini or pappardelle, cooked

Combine the beef, tomato sauce, wine, onions, garlic, bay leaf, thyme, salt and pepper in a 4- or 5-quart casserole or Dutch oven. Bring to a simmer over medium heat. Cover and place in a 300-degree oven. Adjust the oven temperature if necessary to maintain the stew at a low simmer. Simmer for 90 minutes.

Add the mushrooms. Cook until the beef is tender and the sauce is thickened and browned. Adjust the seasonings. Remove the bay leaf.

Serve over the hot noodles.

Yields 4 to 5 servings.

Dorothy G. Adler

Holishkas

The traditional Jewish version of stuffed cabbage

1 head cabbage
1 pound chopped beef
1/4 cup uncooked rice
1 egg
1 onion, grated
1 carrot, grated
1/4 teaspoon salt
1/2 cup lemon juice
1 cup packed brown sugar
2 cups tomato sauce
1 cup raisins

Core the cabbage and blanch it whole. Drain well and separate into 10 to 12 leaves.

Mix the beef, rice, egg, onion, carrot and salt in a bowl. Roll a portion of the meat mixture in each of the cabbage leaves and place in a Dutch oven or casserole. Mix the lemon juice, brown sugar, tomato sauce and raisins in a bowl. Pour over the cabbage rolls.

Cook, tightly covered, over moderate heat for 30 minutes. Reduce the heat. Simmer for 40 minutes.

Yields 10 to 12 servings.

Constance Reiffen

Beth's Burgers

Beth Emery has been with Aramark at MIT for seven years. She started as Assistant Manager at Lobdell Food Court, became Manager at McCormick, then Catering Director for MIT Catering, and is currently Food Service Director for the campus. She has close family ties with the Institute, since her father and brother graduated from MIT.

1 1/2 pounds ground sirloin
1 cup chopped Italian parsley
1/4 cup finely chopped red onion
1/4 cup capers, drained
1/4 cup Dijon mustard
1 tomato, chopped
2 egg yolks
2 teaspoons caraway seeds
1 teaspoon freshly ground pepper
3 ounces mozzarella cheese, coarsely shredded

Mix the ground sirloin, parsley, onion, capers, Dijon mustard, tomato, egg yolks, caraway seeds and pepper in a bowl. Divide the mixture into halves and shape 4 patties from each half. Make small indentations in the center of 4 patties and fill with 1/4 of the cheese. Top each with 1 of the remaining patties and pinch the edges together.

Grill over hot coals for 4 minutes per side or until cooked through.

Yields 4 servings.

Elizabeth B. Emery

Martha's Casserole

1 pound ground round
2 tablespoons butter
2 (8-ounce) cans tomato sauce
1 cup cottage cheese
8 ounces cream cheese, softened
1/4 cup sour cream
1 medium onion, chopped
1 tablespoon minced green bell pepper
4 cups drained cooked noodles
2 tablespoons melted butter

Sauté the ground round in 2 tablespoons butter in a skillet until brown. Stir in the tomato sauce. Remove from the heat. Mix the cottage cheese, cream cheese, sour cream, onion and green pepper in a bowl.

Layer half the noodles, the cottage cheese mixture and the remaining noodles in a 2-quart casserole. Pour 2 tablespoons melted butter over the noodles. Top with the ground round mixture. Chill for several hours to overnight.

Bake at 375 degrees for 45 minutes.

Yields 8 servings.

Veal Piccata

8 ounces (1/4-inch) veal medallions
Flour
Salt and freshly ground pepper to taste
2 tablespoons butter
2 tablespoons olive oil
2 tablespoons dry white wine
2 tablespoons lemon juice
4 to 5 fresh sage leaves (optional)

Place the veal between sheets of waxed paper and pound to flatten. Mix the flour, salt and pepper together. Coat the veal lightly with the flour mixture.

Heat the butter and olive oil in a heavy skillet. Add the veal in a single layer. Cook over high heat until golden brown. Drain the skillet carefully, holding the veal back with a spoon. Return the skillet to the heat. Add the wine. Cook just until the wine begins to evaporate, stirring to dissolve any browned particles. Add the lemon juice and sage. Turn the veal over and heat briefly.

Garnish with lemon slices and fresh parsley.

Yields 2 servings.

Martha H. Harleman

Veal with Raisin Sauce

You can make this ahead and gently heat up the sliced veal in the raisin sauce just before serving. It is delicious over broad noodles or rice.

2 pounds lean breast of veal
2 tablespoons flour
2 tablespoons margarine or vegetable oil
1 (14-ounce) can chicken broth
1 tablespoon lemon juice
1 bay leaf
3/4 cup raisins
1 (4-ounce) can sliced mushrooms, drained
2 tablespoons margarine or vegetable oil
1 tablespoon currant jelly
Salt and pepper to taste

Trim any fat from veal. Rub the veal with the flour. Brown in 2 tablespoons margarine in a heavy kettle. Add the chicken broth, lemon juice and bay leaf. Simmer, covered, for 2 hours or until the veal is tender. Remove the bay leaf.

Heat the raisins and mushrooms in the remaining 2 tablespoons margarine in a saucepan. Stir in the jelly.

Remove the veal from the stock and slice. Add the raisin mixture to the liquid in the kettle. Heat gently. Season with the salt and pepper. Serve as a sauce for the veal.

Yields 6 servings.

Helen Marcus

Cold Poached Chicken Breasts with Tuna-Basil Sauce

A great dish for a summer evening–wonderful with roasted vegetables and rolls or bread.

3 (1¼-pound) whole chicken breasts
Salt to taste
Tuna-Basil Sauce

Rinse the chicken and pat dry. Combine with cold water to cover by 1 inch in a large kettle. Remove the chicken and bring the water to a boil.

Add the salt and return the chicken to the kettle. Simmer for 18 minutes or until poached.

Cool in the cooking liquid for 30 minutes. Drain the chicken and let stand until cool enough to handle.

Remove each breast half from the bone in one piece, discarding the skin and bones.

Chill, wrapped in plastic wrap, for 6 hours to overnight.

Cut the chicken diagonally into ¼-inch slices. Arrange on individual plates. Spoon some of the Tuna-Basil Sauce over the chicken.

Garnish with capers, sprigs of basil, lemon slices and kalamata or niçoise olives. Serve the remaining sauce from a separate bowl.

Yields 6 servings.

Tuna-Basil Sauce

1 (6-ounce) can olive oil-packed tuna, drained
½ cup mayonnaise
¼ cup plain yogurt
3 anchovy fillets (optional)
1 tablespoon capers, drained
2 tablespoons fresh lemon juice, or to taste
Pepper to taste
⅓ cup finely chopped fresh basil

Combine the tuna, mayonnaise, yogurt, anchovies, capers, lemon juice and pepper in a blender or food processor container. Process until smooth.

Chill in an airtight container for 6 hours to overnight.

Stir the basil into the sauce and adjust the seasonings.

Yields 6 servings.

Catherine N. Stratton

Chicken Curry

Chicken Curry makes a festive dinner party, but you must serve condiments such as chutney, salted peanuts, flaked coconut, raisins, bananas, and sambal (an Indonesian hot pepper sauce available in specialty food shops). You need not use all of them, but the chutney and peanuts are a must.

Shirley Saxon is the wife of a former chairman of the MIT Corporation.

4 pounds boneless skinless chicken breasts
1/2 cup (or more) butter
1 large onion, chopped finely
3 cloves of garlic, minced
5 tablespoons flour
1/4 cup curry, or to taste
2 1/2 teaspoons ground ginger
1 tablespoon ground cardamom
1 1/2 teaspoons salt, or to taste
3/4 teaspoon pepper
3 1/2 cups (or more) chicken broth
1 (14-ounce) can stewed tomatoes
2 or 3 apples, chopped

Rinse the chicken and pat dry. Cut into bite-size pieces. Cook the chicken in 6 tablespoons of the butter in a skillet until golden brown. Remove the chicken and set aside.

Melt the remaining butter in the skillet. Add the onion and garlic. Sauté until tender but not browned.

Mix the flour, curry, ginger, cardamom, salt and pepper in a bowl. Stir into the onion mixture. Cook over medium heat, stirring until smooth.

Stir in the chicken broth gradually. Bring almost to a boil. Add the tomatoes and apples. Simmer for 5 minutes.

Place the chicken in a casserole. Pour the sauce over the chicken, adding more broth for a thinner sauce. Bake, covered, at 350 degrees for 45 minutes or until the chicken is tender and cooked through. Serve on rice with condiments.

Yields 8 to 10 servings.

Shirley Saxon

Chicken Mascotti

2 pounds boneless skinless chicken breasts
1/2 cup flour
1/2 teaspoon salt
1/4 teaspoon pepper
2 tablespoons olive oil
1/4 cup butter
2 tablespoons finely chopped shallots
1 teaspoon minced garlic
4 ounces mushrooms, cut into halves
2 (6-ounce) jars marinated artichoke hearts, drained
1 can chicken broth
1/2 cup dry white wine
1/3 cup sherry
1/2 teaspoon Kitchen Bouquet

Rinse the chicken and pat dry. Cut into 1/2x2-inch strips. Mix the flour, salt and pepper in a shallow bowl. Dredge the chicken in the mixture and shake off the excess.

Heat the oil and 2 tablespoons of the butter in a large skillet over medium-high heat. Add the chicken. Cook for 10 minutes or until the chicken is browned and no longer pink. Set the chicken aside and keep warm.

Melt the remaining butter in the skillet. Add the shallots, garlic and mushrooms. Cook until the mushrooms are wilted. Add the artichoke hearts. Cook for 1 minute. Remove and mix with the chicken.

Stir the chicken broth into the skillet, scraping up the browned bits. Add the wine and sherry. Simmer over low heat for 5 minutes. Add the Kitchen Bouquet. Strain the sauce through a sieve over the chicken mixture. Return the chicken and the sauce to the skillet. Simmer for 2 minutes or until lightly glazed with the sauce. Season with additional salt and pepper.

Yields 8 servings.

Louis Ferretti

Citrus Herb Baked Chicken

Baked whole chickens are easy to prepare, and they make a relatively inexpensive meal. The chicken can also be used for salads, crepes and sandwiches.

1 (3-pound) roasting chicken
1/2 teaspoon pepper
2 cloves of garlic, crushed
1/4 cup lemon juice
1/4 cup extra-virgin olive oil
1 1/2 teaspoons dried thyme

Preheat the oven to 450 degrees. Rinse the chicken inside and out and pat dry. Sprinkle with pepper. Rub with garlic inside and out. Place breast side up on a roasting rack. Pour a mixture of the lemon juice and olive oil over the chicken, rubbing in lightly. Sprinkle with the thyme.

Reduce the oven temperature to 350 degrees. Roast the chicken for 1 1/4 hours or until the joints pull away easily, basting with pan drippings every 15 minutes. Remove the skin before serving.

Yields 4 servings.

Country Captain Chicken

This dish has been lovingly prepared for many years by the Women's League members for the International Wives Annual Fall Welcoming Dinner.

1 chicken, or 1½ pounds boneless chicken breasts
4 to 8 slices bacon
1 large green bell pepper, chopped
½ cup chopped onion
2 cloves of garlic, minced
¾ cup chopped celery
2 tablespoons curry powder, or to taste
½ teaspoon thyme
1 (28-ounce) can whole tomatoes, coarsely chopped
3 tablespoons currants or raisins

Rinse the chicken. Boil the chicken in water to cover in a saucepan until cooked through. Remove and discard any skin or bones. Cut the chicken into bite-size pieces.

Cook the bacon in a large skillet until crisp. Remove and crumble the bacon. Sauté the green pepper, onion, garlic and celery in the bacon drippings in the skillet for 5 minutes or until tender. Stir in the curry powder and thyme. Add the undrained tomatoes, chicken and currants. Bring to a boil. Simmer for 30 minutes. Remove to a serving dish. Top with the bacon. Garnish with slivered almonds and parsley.

Serve with rice.

You may bake the chicken until cooked through instead of boiling.

Yields 8 to 10 servings.

Sharon Defty

Mom's Herbed Garlic Chicken

1 teaspoon salt, or to taste
½ teaspoon pepper
⅓ cup freshly ground or grated Parmesan cheese
½ cup chopped fresh parsley
1 or 2 cloves of garlic, pressed
1 teaspoon thyme
⅓ cup Italian bread crumbs
1½ pounds boneless skinless chicken breasts
2 tablespoons butter
2 tablespoons olive oil
⅓ cup water
½ cup white wine

Mix the salt, pepper, cheese, parsley, garlic, thyme and bread crumbs in a shallow dish. Rinse the chicken and pat dry. Dredge in the cheese mixture and place in a baking pan. Sprinkle any excess cheese mixture over the chicken. Dot with the butter and drizzle with the olive oil. Pour the water around the edges.

Bake at 350 degrees for 25 minutes. Remove from the oven and pour the wine around the edges. Bake, covered, for 10 to 15 minutes or until the chicken is cooked through.

Serve with rice.

Yields 4 to 6 servings.

Traci Considine

Oriental Chicken

The brown raisin wine sauce imbues this chicken with a sweet but savory flavor.

2 boneless skinless chicken breasts, split into halves
1 tablespoon cornstarch
2 tablespoons brown sugar
1/4 teaspoon oregano
1 clove of garlic, crushed
2 tablespoons vegetable oil
1/4 cup soy sauce
3/4 cup rosé wine
1/3 cup raisins

Rinse the chicken and pat dry. Pierce several times with a fork. Arrange in a 3-quart casserole. Mix the cornstarch, brown sugar, oregano, garlic, oil, soy sauce, wine and raisins in a bowl. Pour over the chicken.

Microwave, covered, on High for 11 to 13 minutes or until the chicken is cooked through, rotating 1/2 turn after 6 minutes.

Serve with rice.

Yields 4 servings.

Carolyn Latanision

Savory Chicken

6 boneless chicken breasts
1/3 cup flour
1 1/2 teaspoons salt
1 teaspoon paprika
1/4 cup butter
6 small slices cooked ham
1 teaspoon crumbled dried summer savory
Celery leaves
2 cups whole fresh button mushrooms with stems
1/2 cup sauterne
1 cup light sour cream

Rinse the chicken and pat dry. Mix the flour, salt and paprika in a non-recycled brown paper bag. Shake 1 piece of chicken at a time in the bag until coated. Brown lightly in the butter in a heavy nonstick skillet.

Trim the ham slices to fit under the chicken and arrange in a casserole. Sprinkle with the savory and add a few celery leaves. Cover with the chicken. Add the mushrooms.

Stir the wine into the drippings in the skillet. Blend in a mixture of the remaining flour mixture and the sour cream. Pour over the chicken.

Bake, covered, at 350 degrees for 1 hour. Garnish with sprigs of parsley.

Serve with rice pilaf, a green vegetable, individual fruit salads and hot rolls. Serve from the kitchen or by the host, but remember that presentation is vital.

Yields 6 servings.

Joyce M. Baclawski

Pollo Cacciatore

1 (2½- to 3-pound) chicken, cut into 8 pieces
¼ cup flour
¼ cup vegetable oil
¼ cup finely chopped onion
¼ cup finely chopped celery
1 tablespoon finely chopped green pepper
1½ cups chopped canned or fresh tomatoes
¾ teaspoon crumbled oregano
1¼ teaspoons salt
½ teaspoon freshly ground pepper

Rinse the chicken and pat dry. Dust with the flour.

Heat the oil in a skillet. Add the chicken and brown quickly. Remove to a casserole. Add the onion, celery, green pepper, tomatoes, oregano, salt and pepper. Bake, covered, at 325 degrees for 1 hour.

Yields 4 servings.

Adelaide Holley

Chicken Potpie

1 (10-ounce) package frozen mixed vegetables
1/3 cup margarine or butter
1/3 cup flour
1/3 cup chopped onion
1/2 teaspoon salt
1/4 teaspoon pepper
1 3/4 cups chicken or turkey broth
2/3 cup milk
2 cups chopped cooked chicken or turkey
Celery Seed Pastry

Blanch the vegetables for a few minutes or microwave using the package directions.

Melt the margarine in a saucepan over low heat. Blend in the flour, onion, salt and pepper. Cook over low heat until bubbly, stirring constantly until smooth. Remove from the heat. Stir in the chicken broth and milk gradually. Bring to a boil, stirring constantly. Boil for 1 minute, stirring constantly. Add the chicken and vegetables and mix well.

Roll 2/3 of the Celery Seed Pastry into a 13-inch square on a lightly floured board. Ease into a 9x9-inch baking pan. Pour in the chicken mixture. Roll the remaining Celery Seed Pastry into an 11-inch square. Place over the chicken mixture. Roll the edges under and flute. Cut vents in the center. Place on a baking sheet.

Bake at 425 degrees for 30 to 35 minutes or until the crust is browned.

Yields 6 servings.

Celery Seed Pastry

2 cups flour
2 teaspoons celery seeds
1 teaspoon salt
2/3 cup plus 2 tablespoons shortening
4 to 5 tablespoons cold water

Mix the flour, celery seeds and salt in a bowl. Cut in the shortening until crumbly. Sprinkle in the water 1 tablespoon at a time, mixing with a fork until all the flour is moistened and the pastry almost cleans the side of the bowl; add an additional 1 to 2 teaspoons water if needed. Gather the dough into a ball. Roll out as needed.

Yields enough dough for 2 pastries.

Sue Crowley

Charcoaled Butterfly Lamb

1/4 cup vegetable oil
1 cup red wine
1 or 2 cloves of garlic, minced
1 teaspoon oregano
1 teaspoon rosemary
1/4 teaspoon allspice
Freshly ground pepper
1 (5- to 6-pound) leg of lamb, boned, butterflied

Mix the oil, wine, garlic, oregano, rosemary, allspice and pepper in a large container. Add the lamb. Marinate in the refrigerator for several hours to overnight.

Cook over hot coals for 20 minutes per side or until cooked through.

Yields 8 to 12 servings.

Fluffier Eggs

Eggs beat better when not too cold. For best results, they should be at a cool room temperature.

Grill of Peppers and Pork

4 (1-inch) boneless center cut pork chops
Freshly ground pepper to taste
2 red bell peppers, cut into 1/2-inch strips
2 yellow bell peppers, cut into 1/2-inch strips
1 large Vidalia onion, cut into 1/2-inch strips
1/4 cup white wine Worcestershire sauce
2 tablespoons dark brown sugar
1/4 cup white wine
2 tablespoons spicy brown mustard
1 teaspoon dried sweet basil leaves

Rinse the pork chops and pat dry. Season with the pepper and place on heavy-duty foil. Cover with the peppers and onion.

Mix the Worcestershire sauce, brown sugar, wine, mustard and basil in a bowl. Pour over the pork chops. Close the foil tightly and place in the refrigerator until needed.

Place the foil package on the grill rack over medium coals. Open the foil to allow steam to escape. Grill with the lid closed for 20 to 40 minutes or until the pork is cooked through and fork-tender.

Serve on a bed of the peppers with long grain white rice or potato.

Yields 4 servings.

Candace Royer

Grilled Pork Tenderloin

$1/4$ cup vegetable oil
$1/4$ cup dry white wine
3 cloves of garlic, lightly crushed
2 ($3/4$- to 1-pound) whole pork tenderloins
$1/4$ cup dry white wine
1 tablespoon minced shallot
1 cup whipping cream
3 tablespoons Dijon mustard
Salt and pepper to taste

Mix the oil, $1/4$ cup wine and garlic in a large container. Add the tenderloins. Marinate in the refrigerator for 24 hours.

For the gravy, bring $1/4$ cup wine and shallot to a boil in a small saucepan. Cook until reduced to 2 tablespoons. Add the whipping cream. Simmer for 2 minutes or until slightly thickened. Strain the gravy, discarding the shallot. Whisk in the Dijon mustard, salt and pepper.

Grill the tenderloins for 5 minutes per side or until cooked through. Slice thinly on the bias. Arrange in a small semicircle on a plate. Pour a line of gravy down the center of the meat. Serve the remaining gravy at the table.

Serve with your choice of potatoes and vegetables.

Yields 4 servings.

Dan Kurys

Bouillabaisse

$1/4$ cup olive oil
1 rib celery, chopped
1 medium onion, finely chopped
1 clove of garlic, finely chopped
1 leek, chopped
$1/2$ teaspoon thyme
1 bay leaf
2 cups crushed tomatoes
1 cup each bottled clam juice and white wine
$1/4$ cup finely chopped fennel
$1/8$ teaspoon saffron, or to taste
Salt and pepper to taste
2 tablespoons chopped parsley
1 pound scallops
12 mussels, cleaned, beard removed
12 shrimp, shelled, deveined
1 pound red snapper or cod, cut into bite-size pieces

Heat the olive oil in a large kettle. Add the celery, onion, garlic, leek, thyme and bay leaf. Cook for 5 minutes. Add the tomatoes, clam juice, wine, fennel, saffron, salt, pepper and parsley. Simmer for 15 minutes. Add the remaining ingredients. Cook for 15 minutes longer. Remove the bay leaf.

Yields 4 to 6 servings.

Shirley Saxon

Cooking a Lobster

The boiling time of a lobster depends entirely on its weight. Allow about $2\frac{1}{2}$ quarts of salted water per lobster. From the time the water returns to the boil, cook the lobster for approximately 10 minutes for the first pound and 6 minutes per each additional pound. So, a $1\frac{1}{2}$-pound lobster should be boiled for approximately 13 minutes.

Creole Baked Fish

6 catfish or other fish fillets
Creole seasoning to taste
Salt and pepper to taste
1/4 cup vegetable oil
1 large green or red bell pepper
3 ribs celery, finely chopped
2 cloves of garlic, minced
2 (6-ounce) cans tomato paste
1 (8-ounce) can tomato sauce
1 quart water

Season the fish with the Creole seasoning, salt and pepper. Brown in the oil in a large skillet. Place in a baking dish.

Sauté the green pepper, celery and garlic in the skillet. Add the tomato paste, tomato sauce and water and mix well. Pour over the fish.

Bake at 350 degrees for 30 minutes.

Serve over rice or mashed potatoes.

Yields 4 to 6 servings.

Mary Hill

Fish in Soufflé Topping

The fish remains moist and juicy with a crusty, flavorful topping.

1 pound fillets or steaks of scrod, halibut, flounder or other firm white fish
Lemon juice to taste
Salt and pepper to taste
Paprika to taste
1/4 cup mayonnaise
1 egg yolk
1 tablespoon chopped capers, drained
1 tablespoon chopped chives
1 tablespoon chopped parsley
1/2 cup shredded Cheddar cheese
1 egg white, stiffly beaten

Arrange the fish in a lightly oiled or buttered ovenproof serving dish. Sprinkle with the lemon juice, salt, pepper and paprika. Broil for 3 to 4 minutes or until cooked through.

Mix the mayonnaise, egg yolk, capers, chives, parsley and Cheddar cheese in a bowl. Fold in the egg white. Spread over the fish. Broil for 3 to 5 minutes or until the topping is brown.

Yields 2 to 3 servings.

Madeleine Gaut

Broiled Bluefish

This dish can make a bluefish lover out of just about everyone.

Laya Wiesner is the wife of a past president of MIT.

2 pounds fresh bluefish fillets
1 cup mayonnaise
1 tablespoon dry or prepared mustard, or to taste

Arrange the fish non-presentation side up on a broiler pan. Broil for 5 minutes.

Turn over the fish. Cover with a mixture of the mayonnaise and mustard. Broil for 5 to 10 minutes or until golden and bubbly and cooked through.

Yields 4 servings.

Laya W. Wiesner

Spice Rub for Grilled Bluefish

Toast 1 tablespoon each fennel seeds and coriander seeds over medium heat for 2 to 3 minutes. Crush with a heavy spoon on the bottom of a pan. Combine with 1 teaspoon each cinnamon and cayenne; 1 tablespoon each freshly cracked black pepper and dry mustard; and 2 tablespoons kosher salt in a bowl and mix well. Rub bluefish lightly with olive oil and dust with the spice rub. Yields approximately 1/4 cup.

Flounder Monterey

Flounder Monterey is an old favorite for a tasty, at-home, quick-and-easy recipe, yet suitably different for company at short notice.

1 1/2 pounds flounder fillets
Salt and pepper to taste
1/3 cup dry white wine
Juice of 1 lemon
1 bay leaf, crushed
1/4 cup butter or margarine
1 tablespoon instant minced onion
2 sprigs of parsley, chopped
1/8 teaspoon ground ginger

Season the fish with salt and pepper. Cut into serving-size pieces. Roll up and secure with wooden picks.

Combine the wine, lemon juice, bay leaf, butter, onion, parsley and ginger in a skillet. Bring to a boil. Add the fish. Simmer, covered, for 10 minutes, basting with the sauce occasionally.

Serve over a bed of spinach or herbed rice.

Yields 4 servings.

Margaret F. Mann

Stuffed Fish with Tahini (Taratoor) Sauce

This elegant Middle Eastern dish is simple to prepare and is excellent for a buffet. Ask your fish seller to bone the fish, keeping the head and tail intact, to facilitate cutting and serving the stuffed fish. Instead of adding the sauce to the fish, you may serve it separately at the table. Use a baking pan that you can take from the oven to the table.

1 (3- to 3½-pound) haddock, cod, bass or other firm white fish
Salt to taste
1 cup finely chopped onion
⅓ cup olive oil or vegetable oil
½ cup pine nuts or chopped walnuts
½ cup chopped parsley
¼ cup pomegranate seeds (optional)
Pepper to taste
Tahini Sauce

Rinse the fish and pat dry. Salt the fish lightly inside and out.

Sauté the onion in the olive oil in a skillet until tender and translucent. Add the pine nuts. Sauté for several minutes. Remove from the heat. Stir in the parsley, pomegranate seeds, pepper and additional salt to taste. Remove with a slotted spoon and stuff into the fish. Secure with small skewers.

Place the fish in an oiled baking pan and baste with any oil remaining in the skillet. Bake at 400 degrees for 35 to 40 minutes. Do not overbake; it should not flake. Remove the fish from the oven and spoon the Tahini Sauce over it. Bake for 4 to 5 minutes longer or until cooked through.

Garnish with sprigs of parsley, lemon slices and additional pomegranate seeds.

Yields 6 servings.

Tahini (Taratoor) Sauce

2 cloves of garlic
¼ teaspoon salt
½ cup tahini
Juice of 2 lemons
½ cup water
White pepper to taste

Mash the garlic with ¼ teaspoon salt. Combine the garlic mixture, tahini, lemon juice, water, additional salt and white pepper in a blender or food processor container. Process until smooth, adding additional lemon juice or water if the sauce is too thick. The sauce should be thin.

Yields 1 cup.

Yvonne M. Homsy

Baked Flounder with Sour Cream

This has proved to be a foolproof recipe. The amounts are flexible; it's easy and has never failed to please guests.

1/2 cup (about) flour
1/2 teaspoon salt
1/2 teaspoon pepper
2 pounds flounder or sole fillets
1/2 cup butter
Salt and pepper to taste
Paprika to taste
2 to 3 cups sour cream
1/2 to 3/4 cup grated Parmesan cheese
1/2 to 3/4 cup bread crumbs
1 tablespoon butter

Mix the flour, 1/2 teaspoon salt and 1/2 teaspoon pepper in a shallow dish. Dredge the fish in the mixture.

Heat 3 tablespoons of the butter in a large pan over medium-high heat. Add the fish in batches. Cook for 2 to 4 minutes per side or until lightly browned, adding additional butter as needed. Remove the fillets to a deep-dish pie plate or a 2- to 2 1/2-quart casserole as they are browned. Sprinkle each layer lightly with salt and pepper and generously with the paprika. Do not arrange fish more than 3 layers deep. Mix the sour cream and cheese in a bowl. Spread over the fish without smoothing. Sprinkle with the bread crumbs. Dot with 1 tablespoon butter.

Bake at 400 degrees for 10 to 15 minutes or until fish flakes easily.

This recipe may be doubled or tripled. It keeps well in the refrigerator.

Yields 6 servings.

Paula Brody

Salmon Fillet with Leek Beurre Blanc

Donna Freeborn is the Director of Catering for MIT Catering and has been with Aramark at MIT for almost two years. She previously worked at Harvard and for Creative Celebrations.

1 (2-pound) salmon fillet with skin on 1 side
1/4 cup dry white wine
1 tablespoon Champagne vinegar
1 tablespoon lemon juice
2 tablespoons finely chopped shallots
1/4 cup split sliced leeks
1/2 cup unsalted butter, cut into pieces

Cut the fish into 2-inch pieces. Slice down the center of each piece without cutting through the skin. Fold the meat side out, making the skin come together back-to-back in the center.

Sauté the fish on each side in a skillet over high heat until seared. Place in a baking dish. Bake at 350 degrees for 12 minutes or until the fish flakes easily.

Combine the wine, vinegar, lemon juice, shallots and leeks in a saucepan. Cook over medium heat until syrupy. Remove from the heat and cool slightly. Whisk in the butter 1 piece at a time. Serve over the fish.

Yields 3 to 4 servings.

Donna Freeborn

Foolproof Steeping Salmon with Creamy Herb Sauce

This is an ideal dinner party recipe because it takes no last-minute kitchen preparation–which means the hostess can mingle with her guests right up to serving time. It goes well with rice, a tossed green salad and asparagus.

1 1/2 pounds salmon fillets
4 cups shredded mixed romaine, red leaf lettuce and watercress
Fish stock
Creamy Herb Sauce

Rinse the fish and greens in cold water. Measure the thickest part of the fish; if there are 2 layers, measure together.

Pour enough fish stock to measure twice the level of the fish into a large heavy pot. Bring to a rolling boil. Remove from the heat and add the fish, arranging in a single layer or 2 staggered layers to allow the liquid to circulate. Cover securely to retain the heat. Let stand for 10 minutes or until opaque but still moist and shiny in the thickest area. The fish will remain piping hot for up to 20 minutes without overcooking. Remove with 2 large spatulas and drain briefly.

Arrange the fish over the greens on a serving platter. Spoon some of the Creamy Herb Sauce over the fish. Serve the remaining Creamy Herb Sauce at the table.

You may substitute water seasoned with lemon juice for the fish stock. Mix the juice of 1/2 lemon per quart of water with 1/4 teaspoon each dill, tarragon and salt.

Yields 4 servings.

Creamy Herb Sauce

1 cup low-fat sour cream
1/4 cup plain low-fat yogurt
1/4 cup chopped fresh parsley
1 tablespoon minced fresh dill, or 1/2 teaspoon dried
Salt and pepper to taste
1/4 cup capers, drained

Combine the sour cream, yogurt, parsley, dill, salt and pepper in a food processor container. Process until smooth. Stir in the capers. Remove to a serving bowl. Cover and chill for up to 2 days.

Yields 1 to 1 1/4 cups.

Kitty Weiss

Tangy Sauce for Salmon

Mix 1/4 cup dry vermouth with 1 tablespoon Dijon mustard. Brush over the salmon. Broil for approximately 1 minute.

Grilled Rum-Glazed Swordfish with Orange Vinaigrette

With a hint of the Caribbean, this is perfect for summer entertaining.

Richard Walter is a chef at the MIT Faculty Club.

1/4 cup dark rum
1/4 cup molasses
2 tablespoons olive oil
2 tablespoons fresh orange juice
1 tablespoon fresh lime juice
1 tablespoon finely chopped gingerroot
1 tablespoon finely chopped garlic
1 tablespoon chopped fresh coriander
1/2 teaspoon red pepper seeds (optional)
1/2 teaspoon allspice
1 tablespoon cracked black pepper
4 (8-ounce) swordfish steaks
Orange Vinaigrette
Chopped chives to taste

Mix the rum, molasses, olive oil, orange juice, lime juice, gingerroot, garlic, coriander, red pepper seeds, allspice and black pepper in a large bowl. Add the fish. Marinate for 30 minutes.

Mark the fish on a very hot grill to get diamond-shaped grill marks on 1 side. Turn and cook for 1 minute. Place in a shallow pan. Top each steak with 1 tablespoon of the marinade.

Broil for 4 minutes or until glazed.

Serve on a plate napped with the Orange Vinaigrette and chopped chives.

Yields 4 servings.

Orange Vinaigrette

1/2 cup orange juice concentrate
1/2 tablespoon Dijon mustard
1 1/2 teaspoons Champagne vinegar
1/2 teaspoon toasted sesame oil
1/2 cup vegetable oil
Salt and pepper to taste

Combine the concentrate, Dijon mustard and vinegar in a blender container. Add the oils in a stream processing constantly until emulsified. Season with the salt and pepper.

Yields 1 cup.

Richard Walter

Deviled Crabs

2 cups chopped celery
1 cup chopped onion
4 cloves of garlic, minced
1/2 cup butter
2 pounds crab meat
1 1/2 cups bread crumbs
4 hard-cooked eggs, peeled, grated
1/2 cup chopped green onions
1/2 cup chopped parsley
Half-and-half
Worcestershire sauce to taste
Salt, black pepper and red pepper to taste
6 to 8 crab shells

Sauté the celery, onion and garlic in the butter in a medium skillet until tender. Add the crab meat, bread crumbs and eggs. Stir in the green onions and parsley. Add enough half-and-half to moisten. Add the Worcestershire sauce, salt and pepper. Spoon into the shells.

Bake at 350 degrees for 20 to 25 minutes or until heated through.

Yields 6 to 8 servings.

Mary Hill

Soft-Shell Crabs

Soft-shell crabs are now available for a much longer season than previously—from late spring on through the summer. Preparation takes no more than ten minutes, and your guests can watch.

1/2 cup flour
Salt and freshly ground pepper to taste
4 soft-shell crabs, cleaned
1/4 cup olive oil
1/2 cup dry white wine or white vermouth
2 tablespoons chopped fresh tarragon
2 tablespoons chopped fresh parsley
3 tablespoons gin or anise-flavored cordial
2 tablespoons butter

Mix the flour, salt and pepper in a shallow dish. Dredge the crabs in the mixture.

Heat the olive oil in a large heavy skillet over high heat. Add the crabs. Sauté for 2 to 3 minutes per side or until golden brown. Set aside and keep warm.

Deglaze the skillet with the wine. Add the tarragon and parsley. Cook until reduced by 1/3. Stir in the gin and whisk in the butter. Pour over the crabs.

Yields 2 to 4 servings.

Lime-Ginger Scallops with Walnuts

1 pound scallops
1 tablespoon olive oil
1 tablespoon butter
3 tablespoons lime juice
3 tablespoons Ginger Butter
1/3 cup toasted walnut halves

Rinse the scallops and pat dry. Heat the olive oil and butter over high heat in a large skillet. Add the scallops. Cook until golden, stirring frequently; drain well. Stir in the lime juice. Cook for 1 minute. Reduce the heat and stir in the Ginger Butter 1 tablespoon at a time. Cook until a thick sauce forms, stirring frequently. Stir in the walnuts. Cook until heated through.

Serve with angel hair pasta.

Yields 4 servings.

Ginger Butter

1/4 cup butter
2 tablespoons grated lime zest
1 teaspoon ground ginger
Salt and pepper to taste

Mix all ingredients in a bowl. Shape into a log and freeze until needed.

Yields 6 tablespoons.

Seafood Casserole

This is a special recipe from the much-loved wife of a past MIT president.

3 pounds mushrooms
2 cups butter
1 1/4 cups flour
Salt and freshly ground pepper to taste
2 1/2 quarts milk
1 1/2 pounds lobster meat
1 1/2 pounds scallops
1 1/2 pounds shrimp, or 1 pint oysters
1 1/2 pounds haddock fillets, shredded
Grated Parmesan cheese to taste
1 cup dry sherry or other dry white wine

Sauté the mushrooms in 3/4 cup of the butter in a skillet. Melt the remaining 1 1/4 cups butter in a saucepan over low heat. Add the flour, salt and pepper, stirring until blended and smooth. Cook for 1 minute; do not brown. Remove from the heat. Add the milk gradually, stirring constantly. Cook just until bubbly, stirring constantly. Fold in the seafood and mushrooms. Spoon into a large shallow casserole. Sprinkle with the Parmesan cheese

Bake at 350 degrees for 20 minutes. Remove from the oven and stir in the sherry. Bake for 10 minutes longer.

This may be prepared ahead and reheated at 350 degrees for 1 hour.

Yields 24 servings.

Margaret H. Compton

Shrimp Casserole

This recipe became an "old standby" for me to serve at dinner parties for friends or students while living on campus. The many seasonings give it an exotic flavor, and it can be kept in a warm oven after the baking time expires if your guests are late. It can also be made ahead, and the flavor improves with age.

1/3 cup finely chopped onion
1 or 2 cloves of garlic, minced
2 tablespoons butter or margarine
2 pounds fresh or frozen shrimp, peeled, deveined
1 cup uncooked rice
1 (28-ounce) can tomatoes
2 cups chicken or beef bouillon, or canned consommé
1 small bay leaf
3 tablespoons chopped parsley
1/2 teaspoon cloves
1/2 teaspoon marjoram
1 teaspoon chili powder
1/8 teaspoon cayenne, or to taste
1 tablespoon salt, or to taste
1/8 teaspoon pepper

Brown the onion and garlic cloves in the butter in a skillet. Combine the onion mixture, shrimp, rice, tomatoes and chicken bouillon in a 4-quart casserole and mix well. Add the bay leaf, parsley, cloves, marjoram, chili powder, cayenne, salt and pepper.

Bake, tightly covered, at 350 degrees for 1 1/2 hours.

Remove the bay leaf before serving.

Yields 6 servings.

Ann Holden

Shrimp Curry

This is a quick, easy and delicious luncheon or company dish. Leave out the curry and it becomes Shrimp Creole.

2 tablespoons butter
1 cup chopped onion
1 clove of garlic, crushed
1/2 cup chopped green bell pepper
1/2 cup chopped or sliced celery
2 tablespoons flour
2 teaspoons curry powder, or to taste
1 teaspoon soy sauce
1 cup water
2 cups undrained canned tomatoes, coarsely chopped
1 pound cooked shrimp

Melt the butter in a 12-inch skillet. Add the onion, garlic, green pepper and celery. Cook over medium heat for 5 minutes or until tender. Blend in the flour. Add the curry powder, soy sauce, water and tomatoes, stirring constantly. Cook until bubbly; reduce the heat. Simmer for 20 minutes. Add the shrimp. Cook for 1 minute or until the shrimp are heated through.

Serve over hot rice. Garnish with chopped parsley.

Yields 4 servings.

Eleanor L. Haus

Shrimp and Cauliflower Platter

This dish never fails to startle—and then please—those to whom it is served.

1 small head cauliflower, trimmed
Salt to taste
3 tablespoons butter or margarine
3 tablespoons flour
1 3/4 cups milk
1 teaspoon salt
1/8 teaspoon white pepper, or to taste
1/4 teaspoon Dijon mustard
2 tablespoons sherry
1 1/2 cups barely cooked shrimp

Simmer the cauliflower in salted water to cover in a large saucepan for 20 minutes.

Melt the butter in a large saucepan. Add the flour, stirring until blended and smooth. Add the milk gradually, stirring constantly. Stir in 1 teaspoon salt, white pepper, Dijon mustard and sherry. Add the shrimp. Keep warm in a double boiler if not used immediately; do not boil after adding the shrimp.

Place the cauliflower on a platter with some rim. Pour the shrimp sauce over it. Garnish with parsley. Serve with a knife to cut the cauliflower and a serving spoon to divide the sauce.

Yields 4 servings.

Susan S. Forrester

Mary's Cherry Ham Sauce

A sweet, spicy accompaniment for the smoky taste of ham

1 (12- to 14-ounce) jar cherry preserves
1/4 cup honey
1/4 cup red wine vinegar
1/2 teaspoon nutmeg
1/2 teaspoon cinnamon
1/2 teaspoon ground cloves

Combine the preserves, honey, vinegar, nutmeg, cinnamon and cloves in a saucepan. Simmer for 5 minutes.

Yields 1 1/2 cups.

Dijon Sauce for Salmon

1/4 cup sour cream
3 tablespoons Dijon mustard
2 teaspoons fresh lemon juice
1 clove of garlic, minced
1/4 teaspoon dried dillweed

Combine the sour cream, Dijon mustard, lemon juice, garlic and dillweed in a bowl and mix well.

Serve with grilled, broiled, steeped or poached salmon.

Yields 1/2 cup.

Marinara Sauce

3 tablespoons olive oil
3 cloves of garlic, chopped
1 onion, chopped
1 carrot, peeled, chopped
1 (28-ounce) can Italian plum tomatoes, chopped
4 tomatoes, chopped
1 teaspoon salt
1 teaspoon dried oregano
1/2 teaspoon dried thyme
1/2 teaspoon dried basil
Freshly ground pepper to taste

Heat the olive oil in a saucepan. Add the garlic, onion and carrot. Sauté for 10 minutes or until tender. Add the tomatoes. Simmer for 10 minutes. Stir in the salt, oregano, thyme, basil and pepper. Simmer for 30 minutes or until thickened.

Yields 4 cups.

Keeping Pesto a Vivid Green

Pesto will darken soon after preparation if it is exposed to oxygen. Although unsightly, the dark layer is not harmful and can be stirred back into the pesto. One way to avoid discoloration is to cover the pesto with a thin layer of olive oil. Stir the olive oil into the pesto before serving.

Blender Pesto

This recipe comes from my daughter-in-law, Yukiko Gray.

2 cups fresh basil leaves
1/2 cup olive oil
2 tablespoons pine nuts or chopped walnuts
2 large cloves of garlic
1 teaspoon salt
2 tablespoons grated Parmesan cheese
2 tablespoons grated Romano cheese
1 1/2 tablespoons butter (optional)

Combine the basil, olive oil, pine nuts, garlic and salt in a blender container. Process until smooth. Stir in the Parmesan cheese, Romano cheese and butter at serving time.

The basil mixture may be frozen after being blended. Let thaw before adding the cheese and butter.

Serve with hot pasta, chicken or bruschetta.

Yields 2 1/2 cups.

Priscilla K. Gray

$(C_6H_{12}O_6)n$

(Pasta & Rice)

MIT
Women's League

Cannelloni with Swiss Chard and Walnuts

2 pounds Swiss chard, rinsed, stems removed
Salt to taste
1/4 cup butter
6 shallots, finely chopped
1/4 cup Cognac
1/4 cup whipping cream
1/4 cup butter
1 cup coarsely chopped walnuts
3 ounces Gruyère cheese, shredded
2 eggs, beaten
1/4 teaspoon ground nutmeg
White pepper to taste
6 eggs
1/4 cup finely chopped parsley
1/2 tablespoon butter
2 cups milk
1/4 cup unsalted butter
1/4 cup flour
2 egg yolks
4 ounces Gruyère cheese, finely shredded
1/2 cup unsalted butter

For the filling, plunge the chard into boiling salted water in a large pot. Cook until tender. Drain and coarsely chop. Melt 1/4 cup butter in a skillet. Add the shallots. Cook until wilted but not brown. Add the Cognac and flambé. Add the whipping cream and mix well. Add the chard. Cook over medium heat for 5 minutes, stirring constantly to toss. Brown 1/4 cup butter lightly in another skillet. Stir in the walnuts. Add the chard mixture and mix well. Stir in 3 ounces Gruyère cheese. Add 2 eggs, 1/4 teaspoon nutmeg, salt and white pepper to taste and mix well.

For the cannelloni, beat 6 eggs vigorously in a bowl and strain. Season with salt and pepper. Stir in the parsley. Melt 1/2 tablespoon butter in a crepe pan over high heat. Add 2 tablespoons of the egg mixture, quickly rotating around the pan. Cook for 30 seconds per side, turning once. Remove to a plate. Repeat the cooking process until all of the egg mixture is used.

For the sauce, scald the milk in a small saucepan and set aside. Melt 1/4 cup unsalted butter in a large saucepan. Add the flour, stirring until smooth. Cook for 2 to 3 minutes or until heated through, stirring frequently. Add the milk gradually, stirring constantly. Remove from the heat. Whisk in the egg yolks. Season with salt and pepper.

Cut squares from the crepes and place a large spoonful of the filling in the center of each square. Roll up forming cylinders and place side by side in a buttered 8x8-inch baking dish. Bake at 450 degrees for 5 to 10 minutes or until golden brown. Top with 4 ounces Gruyère cheese and 1/2 cup unsalted butter. Serve with the sauce.

Yields 4 servings.

Dave Dannells

Clams on a Grill

Dig for clams at any good clamming beach. Keep them undistributed in ocean water for 1 hour and then scrub well. Grill over charcoal for 2 minutes per side. They will cook in their own juices and open up. Serve with melted butter, allowing 6 clams per person.

Fettuccini Vongole

This is a favorite Nantucket dish, especially when we take the grandchildren to help dig the littlenecks in the harbor. The best time is at low tide when we can wade far out with a clam rake and wire bucket. If you can't dig your own, try to get clams approximately 1½ inches in diameter.

24 littleneck clams
¼ cup olive oil
½ cup white wine
½ teaspoon red pepper flakes (optional)
3 or 4 cloves of garlic, chopped
6 quarts water
Salt to taste
1 pound fettuccini
½ cup chopped fresh parsley

Scrub the clams under cold running water. Combine with the olive oil, wine, and pepper flakes. Cook, covered, over high heat, stirring occasionally and transferring each clam to a covered bowl as it opens. Discard any clams that have not opened within 10 minutes or so. Combine the garlic with the broth in the pot. Cook for 3 minutes or until the garlic is translucent but not brown. Cover and keep warm.

Combine the water and salt in another large pot. Bring to a rolling boil. Add the pasta. Cook for 8 minutes or until al dente, stirring occasionally; drain well.

Add the pasta to the broth mixture and mix well. The pasta will absorb some of the broth. Heat and place the pasta immediately on individual plates. Add some of the remaining broth to each plate. Arrange the clams around the edge of each plate. Sprinkle with the parsley.

Yields 4 servings.

Donald R. F. Harleman

Mushroom Lasagna with Béchamel Sauce

Although pasta makers often say fresh lasagna sheets need not be precooked, the lasagna will be lighter and moister if they are.

1 tablespoon dried porcini mushrooms
1 cup boiling water
1 1/2 pounds fresh mushrooms, wiped clean, thinly sliced
1 to 2 tablespoons olive oil
1/4 cup butter
2 tablespoons olive oil
2 bay leaves
1 small onion, finely chopped
2 medium carrots, peeled, finely diced
2 ribs celery, finely diced
1/2 teaspoon dried thyme
1 tablespoon chopped fresh marjoram, or 1 teaspoon dried
3 tablespoons chopped fresh parsley
3 cloves of garlic, finely chopped
Salt to taste
1/4 cup tomato purée
Freshly ground pepper to taste
1 1/4 pounds fresh pasta sheets
Béchamel Sauce
1 cup grated Parmesan cheese

Cover the dried mushrooms with the boiling water and let stand for 20 minutes. Squeeze dry, reserving the soaking liquid. Chop the mushrooms into small pieces. Pour the soaking liquid through a paper towel-lined strainer.

Cook the fresh mushrooms briefly in 1 to 2 tablespoons olive oil in a large skillet.

Warm the butter, 2 tablespoons olive oil and bay leaves over medium heat in a large saucepan. Add the onion, carrots, celery, thyme, marjoram and parsley. Cook for 3 to 4 minutes or until the onion is tender, stirring frequently. Add the fresh mushrooms, garlic, dried mushrooms and salt. Cook for 3 minutes. Add the reserved soaking water and the tomato purée. Cook until the mushrooms are tender and a syrupy juice remains on the bottom of the pan. Season with the pepper and additional salt. Remove the bay leaves.

Drop 1 sheet of pasta into boiling salted water in a large pot. Boil until the pasta rises to the surface. Remove to a large bowl of cold water. Spread the sheet on a clean kitchen towel. Repeat this process with the remaining pasta. It is important to handle the pasta 1 sheet at a time to prevent the sheets from sticking together.

Spoon 1/2 cup of the Béchamel Sauce into a buttered 9x12-inch baking pan. Reserve some of the pasta to use as a topping. Cover the bottom of the pan with some of the pasta. Spread with 1/2 cup of the sauce, 1/4 of the mushroom mixture and some of the Parmesan cheese over the pasta. Repeat 3 more times. Top with the reserved pasta. Spread with the remaining sauce and sprinkle with the remaining Parmesan cheese.

Bake, loosely covered with foil, at 375 degrees for 35 minutes. Bake, uncovered, for 5 to 10 minutes or until heated through. Let stand for several minutes. Cut into squares. Serve with sautéed artichokes, a green salad and a red wine.

Yields 6 servings.

Béchamel Sauce

3 tablespoons butter
1 tablespoon minced shallot or onion
3 tablespoons flour
2½ cups milk
½ cup light cream or whipping cream
Nutmeg to taste
Salt and pepper to taste

Melt the butter in a saucepan. Stir in the shallot. Cook until the shallot is soft. Stir in the flour. Cook over low heat for 3 to 4 minutes, stirring constantly. Remove from the heat and cool. Heat the milk and cream in a saucepan just to the boiling point. Whisk into the cooled roux. Cook for 15 to 20 minutes or until thickened, stirring frequently. Stir in the nutmeg, salt and pepper.

Yields 3 to 3¼ cups.

Linguini with Artichokes, Shrimp and Bacon

I first became interested in Italian cooking when Martha and I spent a wonderful month at Villa Serbelloni as guests of the Rockefeller Foundation. The villa is in Bellagio on Lake Como, the most beautiful of the northern Italian lakes.

½ pound sliced bacon, cut into 1-inch pieces
½ cup each olive oil and white wine or vermouth
4 cloves of garlic, minced
1 cup marinated artichoke hearts, cut into halves
½ teaspoon red pepper flakes
¼ cup pine nuts
½ cup chopped fresh parsley
1 pound medium to large shrimp, peeled, deveined
Salt to taste
6 quarts water
1 pound linguini

Cook the bacon in a skillet until crisp. Remove to paper towels to drain. Discard the bacon drippings. Add the olive oil, wine and garlic to the skillet. Cook for 1 to 2 minutes or until the garlic is tender but not brown. Add the artichoke hearts, red pepper flakes and pine nuts. Cook for 5 minutes. Add the bacon, parsley and shrimp. Cook, covered, for 3 to 4 minutes or until heated through. Season with the salt. Cover and keep warm.

Bring 6 quarts salted water to a boil in a large pot. Add the linguini. Cook for 5 minutes or until al dente. Drain and return to the pot. Add the shrimp mixture. Heat and toss. Divide pasta and shrimp mixture evenly among heated serving plates.

You may use Sautéed Baby Artichokes (page 100) in this recipe.

Yields 4 servings.

Donald R. F. Harleman

Seafood Linguini

When I learned how to cook, it took a great burden from my mother, who prepared meals for ten people every day. Because I had time to experiment, I tried new meals so we wouldn't be eating "steak and potatoes" every night. Country living provided many vegetables, and, because tomatoes were a staple for canning, this recipe was created as a treat for my family. The seafood was purchased from "the fish man," who came once a month door-to-door.

3 cloves of garlic, minced
1/4 cup olive oil
Hot pepper flakes to taste
1 (48-ounce) can plum tomatoes, drained, chopped
1/4 cup chopped fresh mint leaves
2 pounds medium shrimp or mixed shrimp and scallops
1 pound linguini

Sauté the garlic in the olive oil in a large skillet for 2 minutes. Add the pepper flakes, tomatoes and mint. Simmer for 3 to 5 minutes or until the tomatoes are tender.

Steam the seafood. Cook the linguini until al dente using the package directions. Drain and place on a large platter. Toss with the tomato sauce.

Serve the seafood as a separate dish or arrange on the platter with the linguini.

Yields 4 servings.

Christine L. McGrew

Italian Linguini Ring

This easy, colorful family favorite could certainly be prepared for company. I have substituted tomato paste for the tomato sauce to allow for personal tastes, and I vary the vegetables depending upon what's available.

1 (14-ounce) can whole tomatoes
12 ounces ground chuck
3/4 cup chopped onion
3/4 cup sliced fresh mushrooms
1/2 cup chopped celery
1/4 cup chopped green bell pepper
1 clove of garlic, minced
1 (8-ounce) can no-salt-added tomato sauce
3/4 teaspoon dried whole oregano
1/2 teaspoon dried whole marjoram
1/4 teaspoon salt
8 ounces linguini
1/4 cup shredded part-skim milk mozzarella cheese
1/4 cup grated Parmesan cheese
1 tablespoon melted margarine
1/4 cup finely chopped fresh parsley

Drain and chop the tomatoes, reserving the juice.

Heat a large skillet sprayed with nonstick cooking spray over medium heat. Add the ground chuck, onion, mushrooms, celery, green pepper and garlic. Cook until the ground chuck is brown and the vegetables are tender, stirring frequently. Drain on paper towels. Wipe the pan drippings from the skillet. Return the ground chuck mixture to the skillet. Stir in the tomatoes, reserved tomato juice, tomato sauce, oregano, marjoram and salt. Bring to a boil and reduce the heat. Simmer for 15 minutes, stirring frequently.

Cook the linguini using the package directions, omitting the salt; drain. Mix the linguini, cheeses, margarine and parsley in a large bowl. Press into a

4-cup ring mold sprayed with nonstick cooking spray. Let stand for 5 minutes.

Unmold the linguini mixture onto a serving platter. Spoon the sauce into the center.

Yields 8 servings.

Cleo Schimmel

Aglia e Olio

(Pasta with Garlic and Oil)

12 ounces spaghetti
2 cloves of garlic, coarsely chopped
1/3 cup extra-virgin olive oil
1/2 cup minced fresh flat-leaf parsley
1/4 teaspoon dried red pepper flakes
1/3 cup white wine
Grated Romano or Parmesan cheese to taste

Cook the spaghetti in boiling salted water in a large pot for 7 to 9 minutes or until al dente.

Sauté the garlic in the olive oil in a skillet until golden. Add the parsley and red pepper flakes. Cook for 30 seconds. Stir in the wine.

Drain the pasta and return to the pot. Stir in the garlic sauce. Reheat briefly.

Spoon into warmed bowls. Top with the Romano cheese.

For a more festive dish, add a half package of cooked frozen tiny peas and a bit of thinly sliced prosciutto.

Yields 4 servings.

Pasta with Carrots, Sage and Scallions

This is a favorite vegetarian recipe of our family that meets the Big Three requirements: it's quick, easy and tastes good!

8 ounces farfalle (bow tie pasta)
1 teaspoon olive oil
1 1/2 tablespoons butter
3 medium carrots, julienned
9 scallions, cut diagonally into 1 1/2-inch pieces
20 fresh sage leaves, stems removed
Salt and pepper to taste
Juice from 1/2 lemon
1/2 tablespoon butter
3 tablespoons freshly grated cheese (optional)

Cook the pasta in boiling water in a large pot using the package directions.

Heat the olive oil and 1 1/2 tablespoons butter in a large skillet over medium-high heat. Add the carrots. Sauté for 7 minutes or until tender and golden. Add the scallions and sage leaves. Sauté for 7 minutes or until the sage begins to crisp and the scallions are brown. Season with the salt and pepper. Reduce the heat. Cover and keep warm.

Drain the pasta and return to the pot. Add the lemon juice and 1/2 tablespoon butter, tossing lightly.

Divide the pasta evenly among serving bowls. Top with the vegetable mixture. Sprinkle with the cheese.

Yields 3 servings.

Ann Sharp

Spaghetti with Lemon and Asparagus Sauce

3½ quarts water
1 tablespoon salt
8 ounces spaghetti
6 tablespoons butter
8 fresh asparagus spears, cut into 1-inch lengths
Finely grated zest of 1 lemon
2 eggs
¾ cup whipping cream
2 tablespoons freshly grated Parmesan cheese
⅛ teaspoon nutmeg, or to taste
3 tablespoons chopped fresh parsley
Juice of 1 lemon
Freshly ground pepper

Bring the water to a rolling boil in a large pot. Stir in 1 tablespoon salt. Add the spaghetti and stir. Cook for 6 minutes or until al dente, stirring frequently.

Melt the butter in a medium skillet. Add the asparagus. Cook for 6 minutes.

Combine the lemon zest, eggs, whipping cream, Parmesan cheese, nutmeg, parsley and half the lemon juice in a bowl and mix well. Taste the sauce; the lemon should be subtle, not overpowering. Add additional lemon juice if needed.

Drain the spaghetti and return to the pot. Add the asparagus mixture and lemon sauce and toss. Cook over low heat for 30 seconds or until the sauce thickens slightly and clings to the pasta, tossing gently constantly. Season with the pepper and additional salt.

Yields 3 to 6 servings.

Lemon-Dill Rice

¼ cup extra-virgin olive oil
1 cup chopped onion
1 cup long grain rice
½ cup dry white wine
Grated peel of ½ lemon
1½ cups low-sodium chicken broth
½ teaspoon dried dill leaves
¼ teaspoon pepper
Juice of 1 lemon

Heat the olive oil in a large skillet over medium heat. Add the onion. Sauté for 5 minutes or until tender. Add the rice. Sauté for 2 minutes. Stir in the wine, lemon peel, chicken broth and dill. Cover and reduce the heat to low. Simmer for 25 minutes or until the rice is tender and the liquid is absorbed.

Stir in the pepper and lemon juice just before serving. Garnish with 2 tablespoons chopped fresh parsley.

Yields 4 servings.

Nutted Wild Rice

1 cup golden raisins
½ cup dry sherry
1 cup wild rice
4⅔ cups boiling chicken stock or canned chicken broth
2 tablespoons unsalted butter
1 cup brown rice
2 tablespoons unsalted butter
1 cup slivered almonds
2 tablespoons unsalted butter
½ cup chopped fresh parsley
Salt and pepper to taste

Bring the raisins and sherry to a boil in a small saucepan; reduce the heat. Simmer for 5 minutes.

Combine the wild rice, 2 cups of the chicken stock and 2 tablespoons butter in the top of a double boiler. Cook over boiling water for 1 hour.

Bring the brown rice, remaining 2 2/3 cups chicken stock and 2 tablespoons butter to a boil in a medium saucepan. Reduce the heat to low. Cook for 50 minutes or until all the liquid is absorbed.

Sauté the almonds in 2 tablespoons butter in a skillet.

Combine the wild rice, brown rice, raisin mixture, almonds and parsley in a large bowl and mix well. Season with the salt and pepper. Serve immediately or reheat in the microwave.

Yields 8 to 10 servings.

Classic Risotto

This is a "classic" risotto recipe in the sense that it provides flexibility in adapting to your taste and creativity. Although it requires your undivided attention for about twenty minutes, the results are well worth the effort.

Use some but not all of the following ingredients: 1/2 cup prosciutto, cut into 1/2-inch pieces; 8 ounces porcini or other mushrooms; 8 ounces asparagus, cut into 1-inch pieces; 8 ounces spinach; 8 ounces peas; 2 red bell peppers, cut into 1/4x2-inch strips.

Any of the vegetables you choose to use should be prepared ahead of time. For example, the mushrooms and/or the fresh spinach can be sautéed in a few drops of olive oil and set aside. Asparagus and/or red peppers can be sautéed or steamed until almost done. Fresh or frozen peas should be placed in boiling water for a minute. Mushrooms are good with any of the other vegetables. (A combination of spinach and red pepper makes a great Christmas season risotto.)

Dilute 3 cups chicken broth with 1 1/2 cups water and bring to a boil in a large saucepan. Simmer to keep warm. Heat 1 cup dry white wine in a small saucepan until almost boiling. Cook 2 finely chopped small onions in 3 tablespoons olive oil in a large heavy pot over moderate heat for 2 to 3 minutes or until tender, stirring with a wooden spoon. Add 1 1/2 cups Italian arborio rice, stirring to coat. Add the wine. Cook until the liquid is absorbed, stirring frequently. Add the chicken broth 1/2 cup at a time, stirring constantly and adding more broth whenever the mixture appears to become stiff. Cooking should continue for no more than 15 to 18 minutes or until the rice stops being crunchy.

Fold in 1/4 pound of Gorgonzola cheese, cut into small pieces, the prosciutto and the vegetables. Return to a simmer. The rice should have a creamy but not soupy texture. Add additional broth if needed or continue to cook until the correct texture is obtained.

Serve by mounding in the center of heated plates.

You may substitute 1/2 cup grated Parmesan cheese for the Gorgonzola cheese.

Yields 4 servings.

A Good Soak

To soften dried mushrooms for pasta dishes or risottos, place them in a bowl and cover with sherry rather than water. If desired, the soaking liquid can be strained and used to give added flavor to the finished dish.

Beta Carotene, Anti-Oxidants et al.

(VEGETABLES & SIDE DISHES)

MIT
Women's League

Sautéed Baby Artichokes

These wonderful little artichokes are found in the North End from early spring until June. They are great with pasta.

12 baby artichokes
Juice of 1/2 lemon
1 1/2 to 2 tablespoons olive oil
Red pepper flakes (optional)
1/2 teaspoon dried or fresh basil
3 cloves of garlic, minced
Salt and pepper to taste

Peel any fresh artichoke stems; remove and discard any that are not fresh. Cut 1/3 off the top and pull each leaf off to the very light green part. Cut into quarters and drop into a mixture of the lemon juice and water to cover. Drain the artichokes and combine with the olive oil in a skillet. Sauté over medium heat until tender. Add the pepper flakes, basil, garlic, salt and pepper. Cook until the garlic is golden but not brown.

You may instead steam the artichokes for 10 to 15 minutes until tender and then sauté briefly.

Yields 2 servings.

Jerusalem Artichokes

Jerusalem artichokes are at their best from fall through winter. Look for smooth-skinned, sprout-free, firm specimens with few knobs (which make peeling even more difficult). Store them in a cool place. When cooked, they will look like crusty roasted potatoes, but the flavor is crunchy and almost sweet-nutty. They may be eaten peeled and uncooked in a salad, boiled, sliced and fried like potato chips, steamed, or puréed in soups. They discolor when peeled, so drop them into water with a bit of lemon juice to keep them white.

1/4 cup olive oil
4 teaspoons minced fresh rosemary, or
  1 1/2 teaspoons dried
Salt and pepper to taste
3 pounds Jerusalem artichokes
1 tablespoon (or more) chopped fresh parsley

Mix the olive oil, rosemary, salt and pepper in a large bowl. Scrub the artichokes vigorously under cold running water. Cut into halves without peeling. Add to the oil mixture, tossing to coat. Arrange cut side down on a large heavy baking sheet.

Bake at 425 degrees for 30 minutes or until the artichokes are just tender and the cut sides are golden brown. Transfer to a platter. Season with additional salt. Sprinkle with the parsley.

Yields 8 servings.

Sicilian-Style Stuffed Artichokes

Finger bowls might be helpful after enjoying a stuffed artichoke.

4 artichokes
1/2 lemon
1 1/2 cups fine dry bread crumbs
1 tablespoon (or more) grated Parmesan or Romano cheese
2 teaspoons chopped parsley
Salt and pepper to taste
Olive oil

Cut the stems off the artichokes to produce a neat flat base; rub the cut surfaces with the lemon to prevent discoloring. Slice off the top cone of the artichokes 1 inch from the tip. Cut off the sharp tips of the leaves 1/2 inch down with kitchen shears. Scoop out the fuzzy choke in the center with a melon ball scoop, taking care to remove all the choke but as little of the artichoke bottom as possible. Turn upside down and press down to open up the center.

Mix the bread crumbs, Parmesan cheese, parsley, salt and pepper in a bowl. Stuff into the artichokes, starting at the center and stuffing between the leaves at random. Place in a pot large enough to hold the artichokes snugly upright in 1 layer. Sprinkle with a small amount of the olive oil. Add enough water to reach just below the stuffing. Cover tightly and bring to a boil. Reduce the heat. Simmer for 45 to 60 minutes or until the artichokes are tender and the outside leaves come off easily.

Yields 4 servings.

Josephine Mirabelli

Roasted Asparagus with Balsamic Vinegar

1 pound fresh asparagus, trimmed, peeled
1 1/2 teaspoons extra-virgin olive oil
Salt and pepper to taste
1 tablespoon balsamic vinegar

Toss the asparagus with the olive oil, salt and pepper in a large baking pan. Roast at 500 degrees for 10 minutes or until tender and light brown, shaking the pan every 2 minutes. Remove from the oven. Drizzle with the vinegar, shaking the pan to mix well.

Yields 2 servings.

Minted Green Beans with Red Onion

2 pounds green beans, trimmed
1 teaspoon Dijon mustard
1 tablespoon white wine vinegar
Salt and pepper to taste
1/4 cup olive oil
3 tablespoons minced fresh mint leaves
1/2 cup finely chopped red onion

Cook the beans in boiling water to cover in a large pot for 2 to 4 minutes or until tender-crisp. Transfer to a bowl of ice and cold water to arrest cooking; drain well. Chill for 2 hours to overnight.

Whisk the Dijon mustard, vinegar, salt and pepper in a large bowl. Add the olive oil, whisking until emulsified. Add the beans, mint and onion, tossing to mix well.

Yields 6 servings.

Barbecued Black Beans

1 (1-pound) package black beans
2 smoked ham hocks or 8 ounces smoked country ham
6 cups cold water
1 teaspoon bacon drippings
2 tablespoons liquid smoke
1 clove of garlic, crushed
1 large onion or 2 medium onions, chopped
3 ribs celery, chopped
2 tablespoons (heaping) seasoned salt
1/8 teaspoon cayenne
1/2 teaspoon black pepper
1 tablespoon (heaping) paprika

Rinse and sort the beans. Split the ham hocks into halves or cut the ham into pieces. Combine the beans, ham hocks, water, bacon drippings, liquid smoke, garlic, onion, celery, seasoned salt, cayenne, black pepper and paprika in a large pot. Cover and bring to a rolling boil over high heat. Turn off the heat. Let stand for 30 minutes; this eliminates the need to soak the beans. Cook, covered, over low heat for 2 hours. Cook, uncovered, for 1 hour or until the mixture is thickened and the beans are tender. Add additional seasonings and water during cooking if needed.

Yields 8 to 12 servings.

Richard Hill

Baked Lima Beans

This recipe of my mother's is wonderful for summer get-togethers—a real crowd pleaser.

1 (1-pound) package dried lima beans
1 quart water
1 ham end or cooked bacon, chopped
Salt to taste
1 large onion, chopped
1/2 cup packed brown sugar
1/4 cup molasses
1 small bottle hot catsup
1 small bottle chili sauce
1 teaspoon (or more) liquid smoke
1 teaspoon (or more) prepared mustard

Rinse and sort the beans. Combine with the water and ham in a large pot. Cook until the beans are fork-tender, adding the salt when the beans are almost done. Drain most of the liquid from the beans. Add the onion, brown sugar, molasses, catsup, chili sauce, liquid smoke and prepared mustard and mix well. Spoon into a greased 2 1/2- to 3-quart casserole. Bake at 300 degrees until most but not all of the liquid is absorbed.

You may cover the beans with cold water and boil them for 2 minutes and then let them stand for 4 hours to overnight instead of cooking them with the ham.

This recipe doubles well; use a roaster for baking.

Yields 8 to 10 servings.

Cleo Schimmel

Tuscan Beans

This is good served hot or cold.

1 tablespoon canola oil
1 medium onion, thinly sliced
1 to 2 cloves of garlic, minced
1 (16-ounce) can tomatoes or 1 pound fresh tomatoes, chopped
1 small green bell pepper, chopped
1/4 teaspoon basil
1/8 teaspoon oregano or thyme
1 (19-ounce) can white kidney beans, drained
Salt and freshly ground pepper to taste

Heat the canola oil in a 1-quart casserole over medium heat. Add the onion. Cook until tender. Stir in the garlic, undrained tomatoes and green pepper. Cook for 1 minute. Add the basil, oregano, beans, salt and pepper. Simmer over low heat for 5 minutes. Garnish with 1/2 cup chopped fresh parsley.

Serve with a green salad and whole wheat bread for a satisfying dinner.

Yields 2 to 3 servings.

Anne Berg

Brussels Sprouts with Chestnuts and Maple Syrup

This is delicious for Thanksgiving.

50 brussels sprouts
3/4 cup maple syrup
2 tablespoons butter
1 cup roasted chestnuts

Remove any damaged leaves from the brussels sprouts. Cut an X in the bottom for even cooking. Steam for 10 minutes or until fork-tender. Plunge into ice water to arrest cooking and to keep them bright green. Drain and cut into halves.

Heat the maple syrup in a large skillet until foamy. Add the brussels sprouts, butter and chestnuts. Cook until heated through. Serve hot.

Yields 8 servings.

Helen Marcus

Amish Cabbage with Sour Cream

½ pound sliced bacon
1 head cabbage, sliced
2 small carrots, chopped
2 large potatoes, peeled, thickly sliced
2 tablespoons flour
1¾ cups boiling water
Salt and freshly ground pepper to taste
⅛ teaspoon cider vinegar, or to taste
1 cup sour cream

Fry the bacon in a skillet until crisp. Remove and crumble the bacon. Drain most of the drippings from the skillet. Add the cabbage, carrots and potatoes to the remaining drippings. Sprinkle with the flour. Add the water, salt, pepper and vinegar. Cook, covered, for 50 minutes or until the potatoes are tender.

Spoon into a serving dish. Top with the sour cream and bacon.

Yields 6 servings.

Jeanne Elliott Fullerton

Creole Cabbage

3 tablespoons butter
2 cups thinly sliced onions
1 green bell pepper, cut into strips
1½ cups chopped tomatoes
1 (2-pound) head cabbage, cut into small chunks
1½ teaspoons salt
¼ teaspoon pepper
½ teaspoon thyme

Melt the butter in a saucepan. Add the onions. Sauté for 5 minutes.

Add the green pepper. Sauté for 5 minutes. Add the tomatoes, cabbage, salt, pepper and thyme.

Cook, covered, over low heat for 25 minutes or until tender, adding a small amount of boiling water if needed.

Yields 4 to 6 servings.

Sweet-and-Sour Red Cabbage

This is one vegetable dish that does not suffer from overcooking! No water need be added, as there will be lots of cabbage juice. Some recipes suggest adding a little wine and flour to the cabbage juice before serving, but I usually don't bother.

1/2 to 1 small onion, chopped
1/4 cup sugar
Canola oil
1 (3-pound) head red cabbage, coarsely sliced
1/4 cup vinegar
1 small green apple, peeled, sliced
1 tablespoon caraway seeds

Cook the onion and sugar in the canola oil in a skillet until the onion is brown. Combine the onion mixture, cabbage and vinegar in a large pot. Stir in the apple and caraway seeds. Cook for 1 hour or until the cabbage is tender.

Serve hot or cold.

Yields 8 to 12 servings.

Lisa Steiner

Extra Zucchini?

Convert your surplus zucchini into a tasty soup thickener by grating and drying it. When dry, freeze in small packages for later use.

Celery Stew

A quickly made, unusual stew with good, fresh vegetable flavor

4 cups celery, cut into 1/2-inch chunks
1 red bell pepper, peeled, sliced
1 1/2 cups sliced onions
3 tablespoons butter
1 tablespoon olive oil
1 clove of garlic, chopped
1/2 teaspoon celery salt
4 tomatoes, peeled, chopped
1 teaspoon chervil
1/2 cup chopped celery leaves, lovage leaves or dill
1/2 cup hot broth
2 cups cooked white kidney beans or shell beans
Salt and freshly ground pepper to taste

Cook the celery in boiling water for 5 minutes; drain. Cook the red pepper and onions in the butter and olive oil in a large pot until the onion is wilted and light brown. Stir in the garlic. Cook for 1 minute. Stir in the celery and celery salt. Cook, covered, over medium-low heat for 20 minutes, stirring occasionally. Add the tomatoes, chervil, celery leaves and broth. Cook, covered, for 10 to 15 minutes or until the celery is tender. Stir in the beans. Cook until heated through. Season with the salt and pepper. Serve hot.

You may add additional broth for a thinner stew.

Yields 6 to 8 servings.

Southern Corn Soufflé

2 (20-ounce) cans corn
12 ounces sliced bacon, chopped
1 small onion, chopped
2 tablespoons flour
1/2 cup milk
1 teaspoon salt
1/4 teaspoon mustard
1/4 teaspoon sharp paprika
1/4 teaspoon sugar
1 egg yolk
3 slices toast, cut into cubes
1 tablespoon butter
1/2 cup bread crumbs
3 tablespoons shredded Cheddar cheese
3 tablespoons butter

Drain the corn in a colander. Fry the bacon in a skillet. Pour the bacon and drippings into a 2 1/2-quart baking dish. Cook the onion in a skillet until glossy. Add the flour and milk. Cook until bubbly, stirring constantly. Add the salt, mustard, paprika and sugar. Cook for 5 minutes. Remove from the heat. Stir a small amount of the hot mixture into the egg yolk; stir the egg yolk into the hot mixture.

Cook the toast cubes in 1 tablespoon butter in a small skillet until golden brown. Combine with the onion mixture and corn in a bowl and mix well. Pour over the bacon. Top with a mixture of the bread crumbs and cheese. Dot with 3 tablespoons butter.

Bake at 400 degrees for 20 minutes or until golden brown and bubbly.

Yields 6 to 8 servings.

Maque Chaux

16 ears of corn
1 cup chopped onion
1 1/2 cups chopped green or red bell pepper
Salt and pepper to taste
1/2 teaspoon paprika
3/4 cup butter

Clean the corn thoroughly. Cut the tips of the kernels lengthwise from the top and scrape into a bowl to extract all the liquid.

Add the onion, green pepper, salt, pepper and paprika and mix well.

Heat the butter in a skillet. Add the corn mixture. Simmer, covered, for 45 minutes, stirring constantly.

Yields 6 to 8 servings.

Richard Hill

Cooking and Peeling Hard-Boiled Eggs Successfully

Place the eggs in a saucepan and cover with cold water. Pour in a bit of vinegar or salt. (Vinegar keeps the eggs from oozing out of the shell while cooking.) Cover and bring to a boil; remove from the heat. Let stand in the covered pan for 15 minutes. Drain the water and shake the saucepan back and forth, causing the eggs to crack against the side. Cool with cold water and peel.

Eggplant Rollatine

Keep the rest of the menu light–for example, don't serve this with a hot clam appetizer!

2 medium eggplant
Salt to taste
1 cup flour
Freshly ground pepper to taste
2 eggs
2 tablespoons water or olive oil
1 medium onion, minced
4 cloves of garlic, minced
3 tablespoons extra-virgin olive oil
1 (28-ounce) can tomatoes, undrained, chopped
2 tablespoons chopped fresh basil
1 teaspoon sugar
1 large bay leaf
1/4 teaspoon oregano
1/2 teaspoon salt
1 cup thinly sliced mushrooms (optional)
1 cup (or more) bread crumbs
1 pound ricotta cheese
1/2 cup grated Romano cheese
2 eggs
3 tablespoons chopped parsley
1/4 teaspoon salt
1/2 pound mozzarella cheese, sliced
Grated Romano cheese to taste

Cut the eggplant lengthwise into 1/4-inch slices. Sprinkle both sides with salt to taste. Drain on paper towels for 30 minutes and wipe dry. Mix the flour and salt and pepper to taste in a shallow dish. Process 2 eggs and the water in a blender until well beaten.

Sauté the onion and garlic in the olive oil in a skillet. Add the tomatoes, basil, sugar, bay leaf, oregano, 1/2 teaspoon salt and pepper to taste. Simmer for 30 minutes. Add the mushrooms. Cook until the mushrooms are tender.

Dredge the eggplant in the flour mixture. Dip into the egg mixture, then the bread crumbs. Arrange on baking sheets. Drizzle with additional olive oil. Bake at 450 degrees until tender. Cool on wire racks.

Beat the ricotta cheese, 1/2 cup Romano cheese, 2 eggs, parsley, 1/4 teaspoon salt and pepper to taste in a mixer bowl.

Lay the eggplant slices on a baking sheet. Spread the cheese mixture nearly to the edge of each eggplant slice and roll up. Arrange seam side down in a baking pan or loaf pan. Spoon the tomato sauce over the rolls. Top with the mozzarella cheese. Bake at 375 degrees for 25 minutes or until quite hot. Sprinkle with Romano cheese to taste.

Yields 6 servings.

Susan Lewis

Eggplant and Tomato Casserole

1 medium to large eggplant, peeled, cut into 1/4-inch slices
1 1/2 teaspoons salt
2 tablespoons butter or margarine
2 eggs, beaten
1/4 teaspoon pepper
1 teaspoon finely chopped onion
1/2 teaspoon oregano
1/2 cup cracker crumbs
1/2 cup shredded sharp Cheddar cheese
6 slices tomato

Add the eggplant and salt to 1/2 inch boiling water in a saucepan. Cook, covered, for 10 minutes or until tender. Drain and mash. Add the butter, eggs, pepper, onion, oregano and cracker crumbs and mix well. Spoon into a buttered 1-quart casserole. Cover with the Cheddar cheese. Top with the tomato slices.

Bake at 375 degrees for 25 minutes or until slightly brown. Season the tomato slices with additional salt at serving time.

Serve with a green salad and crunchy rolls or bread for lunch, with a lamb or chicken dinner or as a vegetarian dish.

Yields 5 to 6 servings.

Lillian J. Alberty

Braised Fennel

This is an excellent accompaniment to fish or chicken.

4 bulbs of fennel
2 tablespoons olive oil
1 small onion, finely chopped
1 carrot, finely chopped
1 rib celery, finely chopped
2 ounces prosciutto or ham, finely chopped
1 cup chicken stock
1 bay leaf

Cut the fennel bulbs into halves lengthwise through the flat side.

Heat the olive oil in a large ovenproof skillet. Add the onion, carrot, celery and prosciutto. Cook over medium heat for 3 to 4 minutes or until the vegetables are softened. Add the fennel cut side down. Add the chicken stock and bay leaf and bring to a boil.

Bake, tightly covered, at 400 degrees for 20 to 25 minutes or until the vegetables are tender, adding additional chicken stock if needed. Remove the bay leaf. Garnish with chopped fresh parsley.

Yields 6 to 8 servings.

Eleanor L. Haus

Fiddleheads

Fiddleheads epitomize the coming of spring.

1 cup water
3 cups trimmed cleaned fiddleheads
1 red bell pepper, chopped
1/2 cup pine nuts
2 tablespoons olive oil

Pour the water into a pan with a steamer insert. Bring to a boil; reduce to a simmer. Add the ferns. Cover and steam for 6 minutes or until tender. Plunge the ferns into ice water until chilled. Drain and dry with paper towels.

Sauté the red pepper and pine nuts in the olive oil in a skillet until the pine nuts are golden brown. Add the ferns. Cook until heated through.

Yields 4 servings.

Parmesan Onions

6 (1-pound) Vidalia onions or other sweet onions, cut into halves
2 tablespoons butter or margarine
1/2 cup grated Parmesan cheese
1/2 teaspoon salt
1/4 teaspoon pepper
1/2 cup chicken broth

Place the onions cut side up in a large casserole. Dot with the butter. Sprinkle with the Parmesan cheese, salt and pepper. Pour the chicken broth around the onions. Bake, tightly covered, at 350 degrees for 40 minutes or until tender.

For a cookout, dot the onions with the butter and sprinkle with the Parmesan cheese, salt and pepper. Wrap the onions individually in foil and cook over medium-hot coals for 40 minutes or until tender.

Yields 6 servings.

Mashed Potatoes with Garlic and Olive Oil

3 pounds medium potatoes, peeled, cut into large chunks
6 large cloves of garlic
1/4 cup (or more) extra-virgin olive oil
Salt and freshly ground pepper to taste

Combine the potatoes, garlic and water to cover in a large pot. Bring to a boil over high heat; reduce to a simmer. Cook for 35 to 45 minutes or until the potatoes are tender; drain well. Squeeze the garlic pulp from the skins and set aside. Return the potatoes to the pot. Cook over medium heat for 1 to 2 minutes or until any excess liquid evaporates.

Combine the potatoes and garlic in a large bowl. Beat with a hand-held electric mixer until fluffy. Add the olive oil with the mixer running. Season with the salt and pepper. Serve immediately.

Yields 6 servings.

Sauerkraut

This is excellent for choucroute garnie.

20 pounds chopped or shredded cabbage
1 cup non-iodized salt

Pack the cabbage tightly in a clean crock or plastic container, adding salt every inch. Fit 1 large plastic bag inside another. Fill with a brine solution of 1/2 tablespoon salt to 4 cups water. Seal the bag with a twist tie. Set the bag directly on the cabbage, allowing the bag to spread out to fit tightly in the crock. (The brine solution is too weak to harm the cabbage if the bag leaks.) Cover the crock with a clean cloth. Place the crock in an area where the temperature can be maintained at 60 degrees Fahrenheit. Let stand for 4 to 6 weeks or until fermentation stops.

Pack in clean jars and cover with the remaining liquid, adding additional water if needed. Store in the refrigerator for up to several months. Rinse well with cold water before using.

Yields 20 quarts.

William F. Pounds

Squash Soufflé

1/2 cup flour
1/2 cup sugar
1/2 teaspoon nutmeg
1/2 teaspoon cinnamon
1/8 teaspoon salt
1 package frozen winter squash, thawed
2 cups milk
3 eggs
1 tablespoon melted butter

Mix the flour, sugar, nutmeg, cinnamon and salt in a large bowl. Mix the squash, milk, eggs and butter in a medium bowl. Add to the flour mixture, beating until well mixed. Pour into a greased 2-quart baking dish.

Bake at 350 degrees for 1 hour.

Yields 6 servings.

Deborah A. Wrighton

Squash Beaujolais

3 pounds acorn or butternut squash, peeled, cut into 1-inch chunks
3 cloves of garlic, minced
1/2 teaspoon salt
1/4 cup water
2 slices bacon, cut into small pieces
Vegetable oil
2 tablespoons butter
1 medium leek, cut into small pieces
3 tablespoons sour cream
Salt and freshly ground pepper to taste
2/3 cup grated Emmentaler or Gruyère cheese

Combine the squash, garlic, 1/2 teaspoon salt and water in a saucepan. Cook until tender, adding additional water if needed. Cook the bacon in a skillet in a small amount of oil until golden brown but not too crisp. Set the bacon aside and drain the skillet. Melt the butter in the skillet. Add the leek. Cover and cook until very tender. Mash the squash mixture with a fork in a bowl. Add the leek, bacon, sour cream, salt and pepper and mix well. Spread evenly in a buttered 10-inch round or oval baking dish. Sprinkle with the Emmentaler cheese. Cover with foil with the shiny side down.

Bake at 350 degrees for 15 minutes. Remove the foil. Bake for 5 minutes or until steaming hot and golden brown.

Yields 4 servings.

Madeleine Gaut

Sweet Potatoes in Orange Cups

Sweet potatoes or yams in orange cups have been a Thanksgiving tradition in my Virginia home for many years. As I always had my husband's students in our home for Thanksgiving, I served these because they could be done a day ahead. At the age of five, my daughter began to help me do this dish as her part of Thanksgiving, and now she always fixes them in her own home.

4 oranges, cut into halves
4 large yams or sweet potatoes, baked or boiled
1 egg, beaten
2 tablespoons melted butter
1 teaspoon dry sherry or 2 teaspoons bourbon
Cinnamon and brown sugar to taste (optional)
1 small can mandarin oranges, fresh orange slices or pecan halves

Scoop the pulp from the oranges, leaving a juicy shell. Squeeze the juice from the pulp and reserve. Peel and mash the yams. Combine the yams, egg, butter, reserved orange juice, sherry, cinnamon and brown sugar in a bowl and mix well. Spoon into the orange shells. Top with the mandarin orange slices. Place on a baking sheet or in a shallow baking dish.

Bake at 350 degrees for 20 minutes or until heated through and puffed.

Yields 4 to 8 servings.

Frances P. Elliott

Pear and Turnip Gratin

1 pound purple-topped turnips
1 pound Bosc pears
1 1/2 cups milk
1 1/2 cups whipping cream
1/3 cup minced shallots
1 ounce Gorgonzola cheese, crumbled
Freshly grated nutmeg to taste
Salt and pepper to taste

Slice the turnips thinly crossgrain. Peel the pears and cut into halves. Arrange alternating overlapping slices of the turnips and pears in a buttered 1 1/2-quart gratin dish.

Combine the milk, whipping cream, shallots, Gorgonzola cheese, nutmeg, salt and pepper in a saucepan. Bring to a boil over moderate heat, stirring constantly. Pour over the pears and turnips.

Bake at 400 degrees for 40 to 50 minutes or until the pears and turnips are tender and the top is golden brown.

Serve with game or pork.

Yields 8 servings.

Lee C. Bradley

Pan-Roasted Vegetable Medley

4 medium red onions
1 large eggplant
1/3 cup olive oil
4 small red potatoes, cut into quarters
4 to 6 medium parsnips, peeled
2 large sweet potatoes, peeled, cut into quarters
4 medium carrots, peeled, cut into halves
Salt and freshly ground pepper to taste
2 large red bell peppers, cut into quarters
2 large yellow bell peppers, cut into quarters
2 large green bell peppers, cut into quarters
2 tablespoons olive oil
4 sprigs of fresh rosemary
4 sprigs of fresh thyme
1/8 cup dry vermouth

Peel the onions and cut into quarters with the root end intact. Trim the eggplant and cut into quarters. Cut each quarter into halves.

Pour 1/3 cup olive oil into a large shallow roasting pan. Add the onions, potatoes, parsnips, sweet potatoes and carrots, turning to coat evenly with the olive oil. Season with the salt and pepper.

Roast at 375 degrees for 1 hour or until evenly browned and almost tender. Remove the pan from the oven and increase the oven temperature to 450 degrees.

Push the cooked vegetables gently to the side with a spatula. Add the eggplant, bell peppers and 2 tablespoons olive oil, turning to coat the uncooked vegetables with the oil. Season with additional salt and pepper. Distribute the rosemary and thyme throughout the pan.

Roast at 450 degrees for 40 minutes or until the bell peppers are blistered and brown and the other vegetables are tender.

You may let cool at this point and cover and store in the refrigerator for up to 24 hours. Return to room temperature before proceeding.

Drizzle the vermouth over the vegetables. Bake, covered with foil, at 350 degrees for 20 minutes or until heated through. Increase the oven temperature to 450 degrees. Bake, uncovered, for 15 minutes or until the pan drippings have browned and glazed the vegetables. Season with additional salt and pepper.

Yields 8 servings.

Glenda Tabaczynski

Curried Fruit Casserole

This is colorful and delicious with ham, beef or turkey.

Betty Johnson is the wife of a former president of MIT.

1/3 cup melted butter
3/4 cup packed brown sugar
4 teaspoons curry powder
1 large can peach halves, drained
1 small can apricots, drained
1 large can pears, drained
3 small cans pineapple tidbits, drained
10 maraschino cherries

Mix the butter, brown sugar and curry powder in a bowl. Arrange the peaches, apricots and pears hollow side up in a shallow baking dish. Add the pineapple and cherries. Dot with the brown sugar mixture.

Bake at 325 degrees for 1 hour, basting frequently with the pan drippings. Let cool. Chill for 24 hours. Warm at 350 degrees for 30 minutes.

Yields 10 servings.

Betty Johnson

Fruit Curry

This may be served as a side dish or as a vegetarian main dish.

1 tablespoon olive oil
1/8 teaspoon sesame oil
4 shallots, finely chopped
1 tablespoon grated gingerroot
2 teaspoons curry
2 teaspoons turmeric
Salt, pepper and cayenne to taste
1 cup white wine
4 ounces dried apricots
6 tablespoons raisins
1 cup low-fat coconut milk
2 pears, peeled, cut into eighths
1 Granny Smith apple, peeled, cut into eighths
1 papaya, peeled, cut into 1-inch chunks
1 to 2 medium bananas, peeled, cut into 1-inch chunks
2 cups cooked basmati rice

Heat the olive oil and sesame oil in a medium saucepan over medium-high heat. Add the shallots. Sauté for 5 minutes or just until browned. Stir in the gingerroot, curry, turmeric, salt, pepper, cayenne, wine, apricots and raisins. Simmer for 5 minutes. Add the coconut milk, pears, apple and papaya. Simmer for 18 minutes. Stir in the bananas.

Serve over the basmati rice.

Yields 4 to 6 servings.

Renée Caso

Spicy Cranberry Sauce

A great addition to Thanksgiving dinner

1 (20-ounce) can pineapple chunks
1 orange
4 cups cranberries
2 cups sugar
1 cup raisins
1 cup chopped walnuts
1/8 teaspoon ground cloves
1/2 teaspoon ginger

Drain the pineapple, reserving the juice. Mix enough water with the reserved juice to measure 1 cup. Finely chop the orange peel and pulp.

Combine the juice mixture, cranberries and chopped orange in a 2-quart saucepan. Bring to a boil. Cook over low heat for 20 minutes or until the cranberries burst. Add the sugar, raisins, walnuts, cloves and ginger.

Store in the refrigerator for up to 2 weeks.

Yields 4 to 6 cups.

Mary's Grits

Great for breakfast and brunch

1 cup quick-cooking grits
1 can cream of chicken soup
1 cup shredded Cheddar cheese
1 to 2 teaspoons paprika

Cook the grits using the package directions. Add the soup and Cheddar cheese and mix well. Stir in half the paprika. Spoon into a greased casserole. Sprinkle with the remaining paprika.

Bake at 350 degrees for 35 minutes.

You may prepare this ahead and freeze for later use.

Yields 6 servings.

π and other Confections

(DESSERTS)

MIT
Women's League

MIT Museum Carrot Cake

Warren A. Seamans was the Director of the MIT Museum for many years. His carrot cake was always served at the wonderful Museum Christmas party.

2 cups flour
2 teaspoons baking soda
2 teaspoons baking powder
2 teaspoons ground cinnamon
1 teaspoon ground allspice
4 eggs
2 cups sugar
1½ cups canola oil
4 cups grated carrots
¾ cup walnut pieces
½ cup flaked coconut
Cream Cheese Frosting

Sift the flour, baking soda, baking powder, cinnamon and allspice together.

Beat the eggs and sugar in a mixer bowl until thickened and light yellow. Stir in the canola oil. Add the flour mixture gradually, mixing well after each addition. Fold in the carrots, walnuts and coconut. The batter will be thick and somewhat lumpy. Spread evenly in a greased and floured 9x13-inch cake pan.

Bake at 350 degrees for 35 to 40 minutes or until the center is firm.

Spread with Cream Cheese Frosting.

Yields 15 servings.

Cream Cheese Frosting

8 ounces cream cheese, softened
½ cup butter or margarine, softened
1 (1-pound) package confectioners' sugar
1 teaspoon vanilla extract

Beat the cream cheese, butter, confectioners' sugar and vanilla in a mixer bowl until blended and creamy.

Yields enough frosting for 1 cake.

Warren A. Seamans

Cutting Bar Cookies

To create smooth edges when cutting bar cookies, use a very sharp knife, wiping it clean after each cut if necessary. If the bar cookies contain nuts or chocolate chips, use a serrated knife.

Chocolate Fudge Pudding Cake

This cake, when baked, has a chocolate sauce on the bottom and cake on the top. It's a Wiesner family favorite.

1 cup sifted flour
2 teaspoons baking powder
1 teaspoon salt
2 tablespoons baking cocoa
2/3 cup sugar
1/2 cup milk
2 tablespoons melted butter
1 teaspoon vanilla extract
1 cup packed brown sugar
1/4 cup baking cocoa
1 1/2 cups boiling water

Combine the flour, baking powder, salt and 2 tablespoons cocoa in a bowl and mix well. Stir in the sugar. Add the milk, butter and vanilla and mix until smooth. Pour into a greased shallow cake pan. Sprinkle with a mixture of the brown sugar and 1/4 cup cocoa. Pour the water over the top.

Bake at 350 degrees for 40 minutes. Serve warm or cold with cream or milk.

Yields 12 to 15 servings.

Laya W. Wiesner

Farmor's Light Fruitcake

1 cup raisins
2 cups flour
1 teaspoon baking powder
1/8 teaspoon salt, or to taste
1/2 cup shredded preserved citron
1/2 cup almond slices
2 tablespoons orange juice or lemon juice
3/4 cup shortening
1 cup sugar
1 teaspoon grated lemon or orange peel
4 egg yolks
1 teaspoon vanilla extract
4 egg whites, stiffly beaten

Soak the raisins in a small amount of water until plump. Sift the flour, baking powder and salt together. Mix the citron, almonds, raisins and orange juice in a small bowl.

Cream the shortening and sugar in a mixer bowl until light and fluffy. Add the lemon peel, egg yolks and vanilla. Beat for 3 to 5 minutes or until light yellow. Add the flour mixture gradually, beating after each addition. Add the citron mixture. Beat for 2 to 3 minutes or until smooth. Fold in the egg whites. Pour into a springform cake pan or nonstick loaf pan.

Bake at 300 degrees for 1 hour. Do not overbake. Cool in the pan for several minutes. Remove to a wire rack to cool completely.

Yields 15 to 18 servings.

Anne Berg

Ilona Torte

Ilona was my mother's name, and this is her original recipe.

6 egg yolks
3/4 cup sugar
6 egg whites, stiffly beaten
1/4 cup flour
2 ounces sweet chocolate, melted
1 cup grated walnuts
1 teaspoon freeze-dried instant coffee
1 tablespoon warm water
1/2 cup unsalted butter, softened
1 cup confectioners' sugar
2 egg yolks
2 ounces sweet chocolate, melted

Beat 6 egg yolks with the sugar in a bowl until pale yellow. Fold in the egg whites, flour, 2 ounces chocolate and walnuts alternately, mixing well after each addition. Pour into a greased 8-inch springform pan.

Bake at 350 degrees for 45 minutes. Cool in the pan for several minutes. Remove to a wire rack to cool completely. Cut into halves horizontally.

Dissolve the coffee powder in the water. Combine the coffee, butter, confectioners' sugar, 2 egg yolks and 2 ounces chocolate in a mixer bowl and beat until smooth. Chill for 10 to 15 minutes. Spread between the layers and over the top and side of the torte. Garnish with walnuts or sliced almonds.

Yields 8 servings.

Eva Roos

Lady Van Rensselaer Cake

2 packages ladyfingers
4 egg whites
1/8 teaspoon salt, or to taste
1 cup semisweet chocolate chips
5 tablespoons hot strong coffee
4 egg yolks
2 tablespoons dark rum
1 cup whipping cream
1 tablespoon confectioners' sugar
Dark rum to taste
Maraschino cherries

Arrange some of the ladyfingers vertically around the edge of a 7-inch springform pan. Line the bottom with the remaining ladyfingers, crumbling some if needed to fill all the space.

Whip the egg whites with the salt in a mixer bowl until very stiff. Process the chocolate chips and coffee in a blender for 10 seconds. Add the egg yolks and 2 tablespoons rum. Process for 5 seconds. Fold into the egg whites. Pour into the ladyfinger mold. Chill for 3 to 24 hours.

Beat the whipping cream, confectioners' sugar and rum to taste in a mixer bowl. Spread or pipe over the top of the cake. Arrange the cherries decoratively over the top. Remove the sides of the pan just before serving.

Yields 6 to 8 servings.

Peter Rhein

Newport Cake

At a hands-on cooking demonstration, Peter Rhein entertained a standing-room-only crowd with five costume changes as he described what he called "private chef secrets" gleaned from his days as a Navy cook and Newport mansion chef. He also created this perfect génoise!

6 eggs, at room temperature
3/4 cup sugar
1/2 teaspoon vanilla extract
1 cup flour
2 cups milk
6 egg yolks
2/3 cup sugar
1 teaspoon vanilla extract
1/2 cup flour
Fresh raspberries or other fruit (optional)
Whipped cream

For the génoise (cake), beat the eggs, 3/4 cup sugar and 1/2 teaspoon vanilla in a heatproof mixer bowl. Place over low heat for 30 seconds or until barely lukewarm, stirring constantly. Remove from the heat. Beat at medium to high speed for 5 minutes.

Fold the mixture with a wide spatula in 1 hand and sift in 1 cup flour with the other.

Fill 2 buttered and floured 8-inch round cake pans 3/4 full with the batter. Place on a baking sheet.

Bake at 350 degrees for 22 to 25 minutes or until the layers test done. Cool in the pans for 5 minutes. Invert onto wire racks to cool completely.

At this point, the layers may be stored in the refrigerator in sealable plastic bags or frozen for later use.

For the vanilla custard cream, bring the milk to a boil in a saucepan.

Combine the egg yolks, 2/3 cup sugar and 1 teaspoon vanilla in a large bowl. Whisk until the mixture forms a "ribbon." Add 1/2 cup flour and mix well.

Add half the hot milk to the egg yolk mixture; stir the egg yolk mixture into the hot milk. Bring to a boil over medium heat, whisking constantly. The sauce will thicken when it reaches a boil. Reduce the heat. Cook for 2 to 3 minutes, whisking constantly to prevent scorching. Be sure the whisk scrapes the pan while cooking.

Pour into a bowl and cover with plastic. Lay the plastic directly on the surface of the custard to prevent a skin from forming. Chill until needed.

Split the cake layers into halves horizontally. Spread the custard cream between the layers and top with the fruit. Frost the cake with whipped cream and garnish with additional fruit.

Yields 12 servings.

Peter Rhein

Orange and Almond Cake

2 medium sweet oranges
4 egg yolks
3/4 cup ground almonds
3/4 cup superfine sugar
4 egg whites, stiffly beaten

Boil the unpeeled oranges in water to cover in a large saucepan for 2 hours or until very soft. Cool slightly. Cut into halves and remove the seeds. Combine the orange pulp, egg yolks, almonds and sugar in a food processor container. Process until mixed. Fold in the egg whites. Pour into a buttered and floured springform cake pan.

Bake at 350 degrees for 60 to 70 minutes or until the cake tests done. Cool in the pan.

If ground almonds are not available, grind shelled almonds as finely as possible in a food processor.

Serve with strawberries and crème fraîche.

Yields 12 servings.

Maureen Miller

Juicy

Hard oranges and lemons will yield little juice, but if you cut them into halves and microwave on the highest setting for 15 seconds, they will juice much better.

Ellen's Peach Cake

3 cups flour
1 teaspoon salt
1 tablespoon baking powder
4 eggs
2 cups sugar
1 cup vegetable oil
1/4 cup orange juice
2 1/2 teaspoons vanilla extract
2 cups sliced fresh peaches
1/4 cup sugar
2 teaspoons ground cinnamon
Confectioners' sugar

Mix the flour, salt and baking powder together. Beat the eggs, 2 cups sugar and oil in a mixer bowl. Add the flour mixture and orange juice alternately, mixing well after each addition. Stir in the vanilla. Toss the peaches with 1/4 cup sugar in a medium bowl.

Layer 1/3 of the batter, half the peaches, half the remaining batter, the remaining peaches and remaining batter in a greased and lightly floured tube pan.

Bake at 350 degrees for 1 hour. Cool in the pan for 10 minutes. Invert onto a wire rack to cool completely. Sprinkle with the confectioners' sugar.

You may substitute 2 cups fresh blueberries or 2 to 3 thinly sliced peeled apples for the peaches.

Yields 10 servings.

Ellen Shapiro

Sour Cream Pound Cake

This makes a great birthday cake to serve with fresh fruit or with ice cream and chocolate sauce.

3 cups flour
1/2 teaspoon salt
1/4 teaspoon baking soda
1 cup butter or margarine, softened
2 3/4 cups sugar
6 eggs, at room temperature
1 cup light sour cream
1 teaspoon vanilla extract
1 teaspoon lemon extract
1 teaspoon almond extract
Confectioners' sugar

Sift the flour, salt and baking soda together 3 times. Cream the butter and sugar in a mixer bowl until light and fluffy. Beat in the eggs 1 at a time. Add the flour mixture and sour cream alternately, beating well after each addition. Blend in the flavorings. Pour into a greased and floured 10-inch tube pan.

Bake at 300 degrees for 1 1/2 to 1 3/4 hours or until the cake tests done. Cool in the pan for several minutes. Invert onto a serving plate. Sprinkle with confectioners' sugar.

Yields 12 to 15 servings.

Dorothy A. Mark

Apple Cranberry Tart

2 all ready pie pastries
3/4 cup fresh cranberries, cut into halves
1/3 cup sugar
1/4 cup dried currants
1/4 cup rum or brandy
8 cooking apples, thinly sliced
2/3 cup sugar
1 tablespoon lemon juice
1 tablespoon grated lemon peel
1 teaspoon cornstarch
1/2 teaspoon ground cinnamon
1 egg
1 tablespoon milk
2 tablespoons cinnamon-sugar
1/4 cup apricot jam, melted

Line a 10-inch pie plate with half the pastry. Cut the remaining pastry into strips. Mix the cranberries with 1/3 cup sugar. Let stand for 1 hour. Mix the currants and rum in a small bowl. Combine the apples, 2/3 cup sugar, lemon juice, lemon peel, cornstarch, cinnamon, cranberry mixture and currant mixture in a large bowl and mix well. Pour into the pie plate. Twist the pastry strips together and arrange lattice-fashion over the pie. Moisten with a mixture of the egg and milk. Sprinkle with the cinnamon-sugar.

Bake at 425 degrees for 20 minutes. Reduce the oven temperature to 350 degrees. Bake for 40 minutes.

Brush the jam over the warm fruit between the pastry strips. Serve with vanilla ice cream or whipped cream.

Yields 8 servings.

Helen M. Pounds

Halftime Apple Pie

2 cups (about) sliced peeled apples
1 tablespoon sugar
1 teaspoon ground cinnamon
3/4 cup melted butter
1 cup sugar
1 cup flour
1 egg
1/2 cup chopped walnuts
1/8 teaspoon salt, or to taste

Fill a pie plate 2/3 full with apples. Sprinkle with 1 tablespoon sugar and cinnamon. Mix the butter, 1 cup sugar, flour, egg, walnuts and salt in a bowl. Pour over the apples.

Bake at 350 degrees for 45 minutes.

Yields 6 to 8 servings.

Sandy Lett

Peach and Blueberry Pie

2 cups sifted flour
1 teaspoon salt
3/4 cup shortening
1/4 cup ice water
2 tablespoons lemon juice
3 cups sliced peeled peaches
1 cup blueberries
1 cup sugar
2 tablespoons quick-cooking tapioca
1/2 teaspoon salt
2 tablespoons butter or margarine
1 egg yolk
1 tablespoon water

Sift the flour and 1 teaspoon salt into a bowl. Cut in the shortening and sprinkle with the ice water, tossing with a fork after each addition. Shape into a ball and wrap in waxed paper. Chill thoroughly. Roll half the dough into an 11-inch circle on a floured surface. Fit into a 9-inch pie plate

Sprinkle the lemon juice over the peaches and blueberries in a large bowl. Add a mixture of the sugar, tapioca and 1/2 teaspoon salt and toss lightly. Let stand for 15 minutes. Spoon into the pie plate, mounding in the center. Dot with the butter. Roll out the remaining pastry 1/2 inch beyond the edge of the pie plate. Fold under the bottom pastry, pressing gently to seal. Brush with a mixture of the egg yolk and 1 tablespoon water.

Bake at 425 degrees for 45 to 50 minutes or until the fruit is tender and the crust is golden brown. Cool partially on a wire rack. Serve warm.

Yields 6 to 8 servings.

Anne P. Glavin

Pumpkin Pie with Ginger Streusel

2 tablespoons minced gingerroot
1 1/3 cups flour
2 tablespoons sugar
1/4 teaspoon ground cloves
1/4 teaspoon salt
1/4 cup chilled butter, cut into small cubes
1/4 cup chilled shortening, cut into small cubes
1 egg yolk
2 tablespoons water
1 pound solid pack pumpkin
1 1/2 cups whipping cream
3 eggs
1/2 cup sugar
1/4 cup packed brown sugar
1 1/2 teaspoons ground cinnamon
1/4 teaspoon ground allspice
1/4 teaspoon ground cloves
1/4 teaspoon ground nutmeg
1/4 teaspoon salt
1 cup flour
1/2 cup packed brown sugar
1/2 cup chopped pecans or walnuts
1/3 cup minced crystallized ginger
1 1/2 teaspoons ground ginger
1/2 cup unsalted butter, cut into small cubes

For the crust, combine the gingerroot, 1 1/3 cups flour, 2 tablespoons sugar, 1/4 teaspoon cloves and 1/4 teaspoon salt in a bowl and mix well. Cut in the chilled butter and shortening. Add a mixture of the egg yolk and water and mix well. Shape into a ball. Chill thoroughly. Let stand to soften slightly before rolling. Roll on a floured surface. Fit into a pie plate. Line the pie shell with foil and dried beans. Bake at 350 degrees for 10 minutes. Let cool. Remove the beans and foil.

For the filling, combine the pumpkin, whipping cream, eggs, 1/2 cup sugar, 1/4 cup brown sugar, cinnamon, allspice, 1/4 teaspoon cloves, nutmeg and 1/4 teaspoon salt in a large bowl and whisk until mixed. Pour into the pie crust. Bake at 350 degrees for 50 minutes or until the filling begins to set. Remove from the oven. Let stand for 10 minutes.

For the topping, mix 1 cup flour, 1/2 cup brown sugar, pecans, crystallized ginger and ground ginger in a bowl. Cut in 1/2 cup butter until crumbly. Sprinkle over the pie. Bake at 350 degrees for 25 minutes or until the filling is set and the streusel is golden brown. Cool completely.

Yields 6 to 8 servings.

Dave Danells

Rhubarb Custard Pie

This recipe, handed down from my mother, is at least 75 years old. I have never seen one like it. People who don't like rhubarb like this pie.

2 cups thinly sliced red rhubarb
1 unbaked (9-inch) deep-dish pie shell
1/8 teaspoon salt, or to taste
1 cup sugar
3 eggs
1 cup milk

Place the rhubarb in the pie shell. Sprinkle with the salt and sugar. Beat the eggs and milk in a bowl. Pour over the rhubarb.

Bake at 400 degrees for 45 minutes or until a knife inserted near the center comes out clean.

Yields 6 servings.

Lois S. Harris

Chilling Wine or Beer Quickly

Place the bottles in a large bucket of ice, water and salt for approximately 20 minutes. (For each quart of ice and water, use approximately 1 tablespoon of salt.)

Strawberry-Banana Pie

1 (1-pound) package frozen strawberries
3 tablespoons quick-cooking tapioca
2 large or 3 medium bananas
1 (9-inch) chocolate crumb pie shell, graham cracker pie shell or baked pie shell
1 pint fresh strawberries, cut into halves

Thaw the frozen strawberries and drain the juice into a saucepan. Stir in the tapioca. Heat until the mixture comes to a simmer and is thickened. Fold in the thawed strawberries.

Slice the bananas into the pie shell. Cover completely with the cooked mixture. Arrange the fresh strawberries over the top. Chill until serving time.

For a raspberry pie, thaw two 12-ounce packages of frozen raspberries. Drain the juice into a saucepan. Stir in 3 tablespoons tapioca. Cook over medium heat until the mixture comes to a simmer and is thickened, stirring frequently. Pour into the pie shell. Chill until serving time.

For an open blueberry pie, thicken 1 pint of blueberries with 3 tablespoons tapioca. Fold in a second pint of blueberries. Pour into the pie shell. Chill until serving time.

Yields 6 to 8 servings.

Mabel Nevins

Tollhouse Pie

2 eggs
½ cup flour
½ cup sugar
½ cup packed brown sugar
½ cup melted butter, cooled
1 cup semisweet chocolate chips
1 cup chopped pecans
1 unbaked (9-inch) pie shell

Beat the eggs in a large bowl until foamy. Stir in the flour, sugar and brown sugar. Blend in the butter. Stir in the chocolate chips and pecans. Pour into the pie shell.

Bake at 325 degrees for 1 hour. Serve at room temperature or serve warm with ice cream.

Yields 8 servings.

Carol Orme-Johnson

Nonfat Yogurt Pie

I started making this pie when my husband went on a low-fat diet. At that time, there were no nonfat desserts available commercially. I still make it, because it is not as sticky-sweet as most commercial nonfat desserts. It's a lovely summer dessert, and you can eat the leftovers for breakfast! Dried cereal, fruit and yogurt make a rather traditional breakfast.

1 cup Grape-Nuts cereal
1 cup rolled oats
1 cup cornflakes or other flaked cereal, crushed
2 tablespoons brown sugar or sugar
½ teaspoon cinnamon
Apple juice
1 cup plain nonfat yogurt
1 cup nonfat cottage cheese
1 teaspoon vanilla extract
3 bananas, sliced
Orange juice
Sliced strawberries

Mix the cereals, brown sugar and cinnamon in a bowl. Stir in enough apple juice to moisten. Press onto the bottom and up the side of a 9-inch glass pie plate. Bake at 350 degrees for 10 minutes.

Blend the yogurt and cottage cheese in a food processor until smooth. Blend in the vanilla.

Dip the bananas in the orange juice. Arrange the bananas and strawberries in the cooled pie crust. Pour the yogurt mixture over the fruit. Garnish with additional fruit pieces. Chill for 2 hours or until firm.

You may substitute fresh peaches and blueberries for the bananas and strawberries, substituting ½ teaspoon almond extract for the vanilla.

Yields 6 to 8 servings.

Helen Marcus

Almond and Hazelnut Biscotti

3 cups all-purpose flour
1/2 cup whole wheat flour
1 teaspoon each baking powder and baking soda
1/2 teaspoon salt
1/4 teaspoon ground allspice
1 teaspoon ground cinnamon
1 1/2 cups coarsely chopped toasted blanched almonds
3/4 cup coarsely chopped toasted hazelnuts
3/4 cup packed brown sugar
1 1/4 cups sugar
1/4 cup melted unsalted butter, cooled
5 eggs, beaten
1 1/2 teaspoons vanilla extract
1 teaspoon freshly grated orange peel
1 egg
2 tablespoons water

Mix the flours, baking powder, baking soda, salt, allspice, cinnamon, almonds and hazelnuts together. Whisk the next 6 ingredients in a bowl. Add the flour mixture gradually, mixing well after each addition.

Knead the dough several times on a floured board to distribute the almonds throughout. Divide the dough into fourths. Shape each fourth into a 2x9-inch rectangle. Remove the rectangles to 2 buttered and floured cookie sheets, leaving 3 inches between the rectangles. Pat to lengthen to 11 inches. Brush with a mixture of the egg and water.

Bake at 375 degrees for 25 to 30 minutes or until golden brown and a wooden pick inserted in the center comes out clean. Reduce the oven temperature to 325 degrees. Remove the rectangles to a cutting board and cut crosswise into 1/2-inch slices. Arrange on a baking sheet cut side up. Bake at 325 degrees for 15 minutes, turning once. Remove to wire racks. Cool for 2 to 3 hours or until crisp. Store in airtight containers.

Yields 7 dozen.

Susan Kurys

A Venetian Dessert

So simple and so elegant, especially after a seafood dinner. Just fill small wine glasses with the very best lemon sorbet and add a splash of vodka. Serve immediately.

Apricot Bars

1 cup flour
1/4 cup sugar
1/4 cup butter
3/4 cup dried apricots, rinsed
1/3 cup flour
1/2 teaspoon baking powder
1/4 teaspoon salt
1 cup packed brown sugar
2 eggs, beaten
1/2 teaspoon vanilla extract
1/2 cup chopped pecans or walnuts
Confectioners' sugar

Sift 1 cup flour into a bowl. Add the sugar and butter and mix until crumbly. Pack into an 8x8-inch or 9x9-inch baking pan. Bake at 325 degrees for 25 minutes or until lightly browned.

Bring the apricots and water to cover to a boil in a saucepan. Simmer for 10 minutes. Let cool; drain and chop. Sift 1/3 cup flour, baking powder and salt together. Beat the brown sugar into the eggs in a large bowl. Add the flour mixture and mix well. Stir in the vanilla, pecans and apricots. Spread over the baked layer.

Bake at 325 degrees for 30 minutes. Cool in the pan. Cut into bars and roll in the confectioners' sugar.

Yields 2 dozen.

Kitty Weiss

Cookie Press Shortbread

If you do not have a cookie press, use the tines of a dinner fork.

1/2 cup confectioners' sugar
1 cup butter, softened
1 teaspoon vanilla extract
2 cups flour
1/4 teaspoon baking powder

Cream the confectioners' sugar and butter in a mixer bowl until light and fluffy. Beat in the vanilla. Add the flour and baking powder gradually, mixing well after each addition. Divide the dough into fourths. Roll into 1-inch coils and cut into 1/2-inch slices. Place on a nonstick cookie sheet. Press with a floured cookie press, adding additional flour as needed.

Bake at 375 degrees for 10 minutes or until golden brown.

Yields 3 dozen.

Elizabeth C. Whitman

Rya's Shortbread

This recipe was given to me years ago by a friend. Of the thousands of meals I have served, this is the one item for which people consistently asked for the recipe–dieters included!

1 cup unsalted butter, softened
1 cup sugar
3 egg yolks
2½ to 3 cups flour
Rum or vanilla extract
3 egg whites
1 cup sugar
8 to 10 tablespoons chopped walnuts
9 ounces semisweet chocolate
Coffee to taste
1 jar raspberry jam

Cream the butter and 1 cup sugar in a mixer bowl until light and fluffy. Beat in the egg yolks. Stir in the flour. Add enough flavoring to make the dough of a spreadable consistency. Spread with a moistened spatula or knife in 2 greased and floured 8x8-inch baking pans or 1 jelly roll pan. Bake at 300 degrees for 30 minutes or until half baked.

For the filling, combine the egg whites, 1 cup sugar, walnuts, chocolate and coffee in a double boiler. Cook over boiling water until the chocolate is melted, stirring constantly until blended.

Spread the jam over the half baked layer. Top with the hot filling. Bake at 300 degrees for 15 to 20 minutes or until golden brown. Cool to lukewarm in the pan. Cut into squares.

Yields 2½ dozen.

Paula B. Cronin

German Sugar Cookies

These thin, crisp cookies are traditional Christmas cookies at our house. The recipe came from Germany with my paternal grandmother.

2 cups melted butter, cooled
2½ cups sugar
3 eggs
½ tablespoon molasses
½ teaspoon salt
1 teaspoon vanilla extract
1 teaspoon baking soda
5½ cups flour
Tinted sugar to taste

Blend the butter, sugar, eggs, molasses, salt and vanilla in a bowl until smooth. Add the baking soda and flour gradually, mixing well after each addition. Chill, covered, for 10 hours or longer.

Shape the dough into 3-inch balls. Roll very thin on a floured pastry cloth. Cut with cookie cutters. Place on a nonstick cookie sheet. Sprinkle with the tinted sugar.

Bake at 400 degrees for 4 minutes or until lightly browned. Remove with a spatula to waxed paper to cool.

Do not substitute margarine for butter in this recipe.

Yields 4 dozen.

Charles Niessen

Hermits

This recipe has been a family favorite for years and a special favorite of our best friends, for whom I make Hermits on all birthdays, holidays and other special occasions. A framed copy of the recipe in calligraphy was a welcomed and surprise wedding present for the daughter of the family.

3/4 cup shortening
1 cup sugar
1 egg
1/2 cup molasses
2 teaspoons baking soda
1/4 teaspoon salt
1 teaspoon ground cinnamon
3/4 teaspoon ground ginger
3/4 teaspoon ground cloves
2 1/4 cups flour
1/2 cup raisins
1/2 cup chopped walnuts
Sugar to taste

Mix the shortening, 1 cup sugar, egg and molasses in a bowl. Add the baking soda, salt, cinnamon, ginger, cloves and flour and mix well. Stir in the raisins and walnuts. Press into a nonstick 11x17-inch jelly roll pan. Sprinkle with sugar to taste.

Bake at 375 degrees for 9 minutes. Cracks in the cookies will remain yellow and appear uncooked. Let cool and cut into bars.

Yields 2 to 2 1/2 dozen.

Nancy B. Kocher

M.G.H. Brownies

As an M.G.H. graduate nurse, it was my great pleasure to indulge in these scrumptious brownies, baked up by the Dietary Department of the Massachusetts General Hospital. As a student nurse, the food plan consisted of "whatever one chose to eat"–free of restrictions. Needless to say, it was impossible to eat just one.

4 ounces unsweetened chocolate
1/2 cup butter
4 eggs
1 (1-pound) package confectioners' sugar
1/2 teaspoon salt
1 teaspoon vanilla extract
1/2 cup chopped walnuts (optional)

Melt the chocolate and butter in a double boiler over simmering water. Let cool. Beat the eggs and confectioners' sugar at low speed in a mixer bowl. Add the salt, vanilla, chocolate mixture and walnuts and mix well. Spread evenly in a greased 2-quart glass baking dish.

Bake at 360 degrees for 23 minutes or until the brownies test done.

These are best baked 1 day ahead.

Yields 20 large brownies.

Barbara L. Connor

Oh Henry Bars

2/3 cup margarine or butter, softened
1 cup packed brown sugar
4 cups quick-cooking oats
1/2 cup light corn syrup
2 teaspoons vanilla extract
1 cup semisweet chocolate chips
2/3 cup chunky peanut butter

Cream the margarine and brown sugar in a mixer bowl until light and fluffy. Add the oats, corn syrup and vanilla and mix well. Press into a greased 9x13-inch baking pan. Bake at 350 degrees for 15 to 25 minutes or until the layer tests done. Let cool.

Melt the chocolate chips and peanut butter in a double boiler over simmering water. Spread over the baked layer. Let stand until set and cut into bars.

Yields 1 1/2 to 2 dozen.

Jean Hull

Molasses Cookies

1 3/4 cups flour
1/2 teaspoon ground cloves
1/2 teaspoon ground ginger
1 teaspoon ground cinnamon
1/2 teaspoon salt
1/2 teaspoon baking soda
3/4 cup melted unsalted butter
1 cup sugar
1/4 cup molasses
1 egg, lightly beaten

Sift the flour, cloves, ginger, cinnamon, salt and baking soda together. Mix the butter, sugar and molasses in a large bowl. Beat in the egg. Add the flour mixture gradually, mixing well after each addition. Drop by tablespoonfuls 3 inches apart onto a foil-lined cookie sheet.

Bake at 350 degrees for 8 to 10 minutes or until the cookies begin to darken. Cool on the cookie sheet.

Yields 1 dozen.

Pat and John Deutch

Taffy Dip for Apples

8 ounces cream cheese, softened
1 teaspoon vanilla extract
1/4 cup sugar
3/4 cup packed brown sugar
1/2 cup salted cocktail peanuts

Combine the cream cheese, vanilla, sugar, brown sugar and peanuts in a food processor. Process until mixed.

Serve with slices of apple dipped in lemon juice.

Yields 1 1/2 cups.

Baked Bananas

Bananas
Rum
Brown sugar
Chopped pecans or walnuts

Peel the bananas and cut into halves. Slice lengthwise and place in a baking dish. Pour a small amount of rum over the bananas. Sprinkle with the brown sugar and pecans.

Bake, covered, at 350 degrees for 20 minutes or until tender.

Yield is variable.

Miniature Cheesecakes

These are nice for picnics or buffets, and freeze well.

20 to 25 vanilla wafers, broken into pieces
16 ounces cream cheese, softened
3/4 cup sugar
2 eggs
1 tablespoon lemon juice
1 teaspoon vanilla extract

Place the vanilla wafer pieces in paper-lined miniature muffin cups. Mix the cream cheese and sugar in a bowl. Add the eggs, lemon juice and vanilla and mix well. Pour into the muffin cups.

Bake at 275 degrees for 20 to 25 minutes. Let cool. Chill until serving time.

Yields 20 to 25 servings.

Julia A. Kaufmann

Toasting Nuts

Spread nuts in a single layer on a baking sheet. Bake in a 350-degree oven or toaster oven until golden brown. Watch carefully while the nuts are toasting—don't even answer the door or phone!

Chocolate Almond Delight

A chocolate mousse dessert made with tofu—but you can keep this a secret if you like!

2½ cups toasted almonds
1 cup graham cracker crumbs or chocolate crumbs
2 tablespoons maple syrup
¼ cup butter or margarine
⅛ teaspoon almond extract
3 cups semisweet chocolate chips
1½ teaspoons vanilla extract
1½ teaspoons almond extract
2 (10-ounce) packages tofu
1 cup fresh or frozen raspberries
1 cup AllFruit raspberry jam
Apple juice

Combine the almonds, crumbs, syrup, butter and ⅛ teaspoon almond extract in a food processor container. Process until mixed. Press into a 10-inch springform pan.

Combine the chocolate chips, vanilla and 1½ teaspoons almond extract in a saucepan. Cook until the chocolate is melted, stirring frequently. Rinse the tofu in a strainer under running water. Combine with the chocolate mixture in a food processor. Process until mixed. Pour into the prepared pan. Chill until set.

Combine the raspberries, jam and a small amount of apple juice to moisten in a food processor container. Process until of a pouring consistency. Pour over the chocolate mixture before serving.

Yields 6 to 8 servings.

Jacquelyn H. Ward

Marquis de Chocolat

1 1/3 cups semisweet chocolate chips
1 cup unsalted butter
1 tablespoon superfine sugar
6 egg yolks
6 egg whites
1 teaspoon superfine sugar
2 teaspoons Grand Marnier
Finely shaved chocolate

Combine the chocolate chips, butter and 1 tablespoon sugar in a saucepan. Cook over low heat until the chocolate and butter are melted and the sugar is dissolved, stirring constantly.

Beat the egg yolks in a large mixer bowl. Add the chocolate mixture gradually, beating well after each addition. Beat at high speed for 10 minutes.

Beat the egg whites in a medium mixer bowl until stiff peaks form. Beat in 1 teaspoon sugar. Fold into the chocolate mixture. Add the liqueur. Beat at high speed for 10 minutes. Pour into a buttered 2-quart soufflé dish. Chill for 12 hours.

Dip the bottom and side of the soufflé dish in hot water 2 hours before serving time. Loosen the edge of the mold with a sharp knife. Invert onto a serving plate. Smooth the surface with a knife. Cover with the shaved chocolate.

Chill until serving time.

Yields 10 to 12 servings.

Aud Kaalstad

Peppermint Pie

1 1/4 cups fine chocolate cookie crumbs
1/3 cup melted butter or margarine
1 tablespoon unflavored gelatin
1/2 cup cold water
3 egg whites
1/2 cup sugar
1/8 teaspoon salt
1/2 teaspoon vanilla extract
1 cup whipping cream, whipped
1 cup crushed peppermint candy

Mix the cookie crumbs and butter in a bowl. Press into a 9-inch pie plate. Chill until set.

Soften the gelatin in the cold water. Mix with a small amount of hot water in a bowl, stirring until dissolved. Let cool slightly and set aside; do not chill.

Beat the egg whites in a mixer bowl until soft peaks form. Add the sugar 2 tablespoons at a time, beating constantly until mixed. Stir in the salt and vanilla. Fold in the gelatin mixture, whipped cream and peppermint candy. Spoon into the crust. Chill for 4 hours or longer.

Sprinkle with additional candy. The candy will melt slightly and resemble little tunnels when served.

Yields 6 to 8 servings.

Windows on the World White Chocolate Mousse

A white chocolate cloud floats over a dark chocolate base in this dessert.

David S. Ferriero is Associate Director for Public Services, Massachusetts Institute of Technology Libraries.

12 ounces white chocolate, chopped into small pieces
3 cups whipping cream
4 egg yolks
3/4 cup sugar
2 envelopes unflavored gelatin
1/2 cup cold water
3 tablespoons butter
6 tablespoons sugar
1 1/2 cups whipping cream
4 cups dark semisweet chocolate chips
1 1/2 tablespoons Grand Marnier or other liqueur

Melt the white chocolate in a double boiler over simmering water. Cool to room temperature.

Beat 3 cups whipping cream in a mixer bowl until stiff peaks form. Chill until needed.

Beat the egg yolks and 3/4 cup sugar in a mixer bowl until the mixture is pale yellow and has tripled in volume.

Soften the gelatin in the cold water in a saucepan. Heat slightly to dissolve, stirring constantly. Cool slightly.

Stir a small amount of the egg yolk mixture into the gelatin; stir the gelatin into the egg yolk mixture, beating constantly. Add the melted white chocolate 1/3 at a time, beating constantly at low speed. Add the whipped cream gradually, stirring well after each addition. Pour into an 8-cup dome-shaped mold. Chill for 1 1/2 hours or longer.

Bring the butter, 6 tablespoons sugar and 1 1/2 cups whipping cream to a boil in a saucepan. Add the chocolate chips. Remove from the heat and stir until the chocolate is melted. Cool at room temperature for 1 hour. Chill until hardened. Beat the chocolate mixture with the Grand Marnier in a mixer bowl until softened.

Spread the dark chocolate mixture evenly over the white chocolate mixture in the mold. Chill until set. At serving time, place the mold in warm water for 5 seconds. Invert onto a serving platter.

Yields 8 to 10 servings.

David S. Ferriero

Coffee Flan

This rich, coffee-flavored custard, a variation of flan, has a caramel topping.

1/3 cup sugar
4 teaspoons instant coffee
1/2 cup warm water
6 eggs
7 tablespoons sugar
1 1/2 cups milk
1/2 teaspoon vanilla extract
1/4 teaspoon ground cinnamon

Set a 1 1/4x9-inch pie plate in a slightly larger pan. Hold down the pie plate to keep it from floating; fill the outer pan with just enough hot water to come up around the pie plate. Remove the pie plate and place the pan of water in a 350-degree oven.

Heat 1/3 cup sugar in a small skillet over medium heat until dissolved and caramelized, shaking and tilting the skillet instead of stirring. Pour into the pie plate. Tilt the pie plate to let the syrup flow over the bottom and slightly up the side. If the syrup hardens, place the pie plate over medium heat until the syrup is softened enough to proceed.

Dissolve the coffee powder in the water. Beat the eggs and 7 tablespoons sugar in a bowl. Add the milk, coffee, vanilla and cinnamon and mix well.

Set the pie plate in the hot water bath in the oven. Pour in the egg mixture.

Bake at 350 degrees for 20 minutes or until a crevice 3/8 inch deep forms when gently pushed with the back of a spoon halfway between the plate rim and the center of the pie.

Remove the pie plate from the hot water bath. Chill thoroughly. Loosen the edge of the custard with a knife. Cover with a rimmed plate and invert the flan onto the plate.

Yields 6 servings.

Anne's Cookie Balls

1 cup butter
1 cup packed brown sugar
1 cup flaked coconut
2 packages chopped dates
1 cup chopped pecans or walnuts
4 to 5 cups crisp rice cereal
Confectioners' sugar

Bring the butter, brown sugar, coconut and dates to a boil in a saucepan. Boil for 5 minutes. Pour over the pecans and cereal in a bowl and mix well. Chill thoroughly.

Shape into balls and roll in the confectioners' sugar.

Yields 4 to 5 dozen.

Crème Brûlée

3 cups whipping cream
6 tablespoons sugar
6 egg yolks
2 teaspoons vanilla extract
1/2 cup packed light brown sugar

Heat the whipping cream over boiling water in a double boiler. Stir in the sugar.

Beat the egg yolks in a bowl until light. Stir a small amount of the hot mixture into the egg yolks; stir the egg yolks into the hot mixture. Stir in the vanilla. Strain into a baking dish.

Place the dish in a pan containing 1 inch of hot water. Bake at 300 degrees for 35 minutes or until a knife inserted near the center comes out clean. Do not overbake; the custard will continue to cook when it is removed from the oven. Let cool. Chill thoroughly.

Cover the surface of the custard with the brown sugar. Set the dish on a pan of crushed ice. Broil until the brown sugar is dissolved. Serve immediately or chill and serve cold.

Yields 6 to 8 servings.

Elizabeth C. Whitman

Crushed Ice

For a really quick way to have crushed ice, run cold water into a large freezer bag and knot it tightly. Lay on a baking sheet so that the water runs into a thin layer. Freeze on the baking sheet. Drop the bag on the floor once or twice; then dip out the ice. A great solution for broiling the Crème Brûlée.

Eclair Dessert

2 (3-ounce) packages vanilla instant pudding mix
3 cups milk
8 ounces whipped topping
21 graham crackers
2 packages pre-melted unsweetened chocolate
3 tablespoons butter, softened
3 tablespoons milk
1 1/2 cups confectioners' sugar
1 teaspoon vanilla extract
2 teaspoons light corn syrup

Combine the pudding mix and 3 cups milk in a bowl and mix well. Fold in the whipped topping. Layer 1/3 of the graham crackers, half the pudding mixture, half the remaining graham crackers, remaining pudding mixture and remaining graham crackers in a buttered 9x13-inch dish.

Mix the chocolate, butter, 3 tablespoons milk, confectioners' sugar, vanilla and corn syrup in a bowl. Spread over the graham crackers. Chill until serving time.

This is best when prepared a day ahead.

Yields 12 servings.

Connie Delaney

Baked Dried Turkish Figs

There is a short season for dried Turkish figs. You may use others in this recipe, but they are not quite as tasty.

Dried Turkish figs
Large walnuts
Dark rum
Confectioners' sugar (optional)

Cut each fig halfway through the center. Insert a walnut into the opening. Place in a shallow baking pan. Pour a small amount of rum over the figs.

Bake at 325 degrees for 15 to 20 minutes or until cooked through. Sprinkle with the confectioners' sugar.

Yield is variable.

Soft Gingerbread

This is really good with a dollop of whipped cream. Just leave it in the loaf pan to slice it if you wish.

2 cups flour
1 teaspoon baking soda
1/2 teaspoon salt
1 teaspoon ground cinnamon
1 teaspoon ground cloves
1 teaspoon ground ginger
1/2 cup butter, softened
1 cup sugar or packed brown sugar
2 eggs
1/2 cup boiling water
1/2 cup molasses

Sift the flour twice. Sift the flour, baking soda, salt, cinnamon, cloves and ginger together.

Cream the butter and sugar in a mixer bowl until light and fluffy. Beat in the eggs.

Mix the boiling water and molasses in a bowl. Add the molasses mixture and the flour mixture alternately to the creamed mixture, beating well after each addition. Pour into a greased 5x8-inch loaf pan.

Bake at 350 degrees for 1 hour and 10 minutes or until the loaf tests done.

Yields 12 servings.

Carolyn Latanision

Vanilla Soufflé with Pistachio Nuts

Jill K. Conway is a visiting professor in the Science Technology & Society Program at MIT.

4 teaspoons unflavored gelatin
1/4 cup cold water
6 egg yolks
3/4 cup superfine sugar
2 teaspoons vanilla extract
1 1/4 cups whipping cream
6 egg whites, stiffly beaten
3/4 cup whipping cream
2 tablespoons chopped peeled pistachio nuts

Cut a double strip of waxed paper long enough to fit around a 6 1/2-inch soufflé dish and wide enough to stand 2 inches above the dish. Secure the collar firmly and place the dish on a flat plate.

Sprinkle the gelatin over the cold water in a bowl. Let stand for 2 minutes. Place the bowl in a saucepan of hot water. Heat gently until the gelatin dissolves.

Beat the egg yolks, sugar and vanilla in a mixer bowl until thick. Beat 1 1/4 cups whipping cream in a mixer bowl until soft peaks form. Stir a small amount of the gelatin into the egg yolks; stir the egg yolks into the gelatin. Fold in the whipped cream. Fold in the egg whites quickly. Pour into the prepared dish. Chill for 2 hours or until set.

Remove the collar carefully. Coat the side of the soufflé with the chopped nuts.

Beat 3/4 cup whipping cream in a mixer bowl until thickened. Spoon into a small pastry bag fitted with a small star tip. Pipe rosettes around the top edge of the soufflé. Garnish with whole pistachio nuts. Chill until serving time.

Yields 8 servings.

Jill K. Conway

Lemon Bread

2 1/4 cups flour
1 1/2 teaspoons baking powder
1/8 teaspoon salt (optional)
9 tablespoons unsalted butter, softened
1 cup sugar
3 eggs
3/4 cup milk
Grated zest of 1 lemon
3/4 cup sugar
1/3 cup fresh lemon juice

Sift the flour, baking powder and salt together.

Cream the butter and 1 cup sugar in a mixer bowl until light and fluffy. Beat in the eggs 1 at a time.

Add the flour mixture and the milk alternately to the creamed mixture, beating well after each addition. Blend in the lemon zest. Pour into a greased and lightly floured large loaf pan.

Bake at 350 degrees for 50 to 60 minutes or until a wooden pick inserted near the center comes out clean. Cool slightly. Remove to a plate. Pierce the loaf several times. Pour a mixture of 3/4 cup sugar and lemon juice over the loaf. Let cool before slicing.

Yields 12 to 15 servings.

Bora Mikic

Fat-Free Chocolate Sauce

For those who crave a delicious fudge-like sauce with zero grams of fat, this is the answer. Guests always request the recipe.

3/4 cup sugar
1/3 cup baking cocoa
4 teaspoons cornstarch
1/2 cup evaporated skim milk
1 teaspoon vanilla extract

Combine the sugar, cocoa and cornstarch in a saucepan. Stir in the evaporated milk. Cook over medium heat until thickened and bubbly, stirring constantly. Cook for 2 minutes longer. Remove from the heat. Stir in the vanilla. Cool slightly.

Serve over ice cream, frozen yogurt or cake.

Yields 6 servings.

Broiled Grapefruit

Grapefruit
Cointreau
Brown sugar (optional)

Cut each grapefruit into halves and section with a grapefruit knife. Remove all the seeds. Pour a small amount of Cointreau over each half and sprinkle with 1/2 teaspoon brown sugar. Place on a broiler pan.

Broil until light brown. Serve immediately.

Yield is variable.

Prune Clafouti

The first visitors I served this clafouti were Italian. They enjoyed it tremendously, as it reminded them of their grandmother's baking a similar dish, and they hadn't eaten it since. Since that first time, I've served it to people of various nationalities. Everyone seems to enjoy its light texture. I use it as a standby dessert as it's easy, surefire and good in all seasons. I've also passed the recipe on to people around the globe.

2 tablespoons sugar
1 1/2 cups pitted prunes
3 eggs
1 tablespoon vanilla extract
6 tablespoons sugar
1/4 cup flour
1 cup milk
1 cup whipping cream

Sprinkle 2 tablespoons sugar in a ceramic or glass pie plate or quiche dish, tilting to coat. Top with the prunes.

Combine the eggs, vanilla and 6 tablespoons sugar in a blender container. Process until smooth. Add the flour and blend briefly. Add the milk and whipping cream. Process until well mixed. Pour over the prunes.

Bake at 375 degrees for 45 minutes or until puffy and brown. Cool for 15 minutes before serving.

Yields 6 servings.

Caroline J. Mei

Global Cuisine

(GLOBAL)

MIT
Women's League

Vatrushka Bread

This is a 15th century Russian recipe that is served in Russian homes for breakfast or tea time.

1 (1/4-ounce) envelope dry yeast
1 teaspoon sugar
1/2 cup lukewarm water
1 cup warm milk
1 egg yolk
1/2 cup butter or margarine, softened
1 tablespoon sour cream
5 teaspoons sugar
2 tablespoons olive oil
3 1/2 cups flour
1 pound ricotta cheese
1/2 cup sugar
2 eggs
1 teaspoon baking powder
1/2 cup raisins
2 to 3 teaspoons vanilla extract

Dissolve the yeast and 1 teaspoon sugar in the water in a mixer bowl. Add the next 6 ingredients and mix well. Add the flour gradually, mixing well until a soft dough forms. Cover and let rise in a warm place for 1 to 1 1/2 hours or until doubled in bulk.

Combine the ricotta cheese, 1/2 cup sugar, eggs, baking powder, raisins and vanilla in a bowl and mix well.

Roll the dough into a 15-inch circle on a floured surface. Spread the cheese mixture over the dough into a 12-inch circle. Bring the edge to the center and pinch to close. Turn over onto a buttered and floured baking sheet. (To ease inversion, dough can be rolled onto a floured bread board or other baking sheet and filled. Place buttered and floured baking sheet on top of the dough. Holding both sheets, with dough in between, turn over.) Open the top of the dough by making a hole in the surface; pull back the dough to form a 2- to 3-inch opening.

Place in a 450-degree oven. Reduce the oven temperature to 375 degrees. Bake for 40 minutes or until light brown.

Yields 10 servings.

Vera Grosberg

Hummus Dip

1 can chickpeas, drained
3 tablespoons tahini paste
Juice of 1 lemon
Salt and pepper to taste
1 large clove of garlic

Combine the chickpeas, tahini paste, lemon juice, salt, pepper and garlic in a blender or food processor container. Process until smooth, adding a small amount of cold water if needed.

Serve with pita bread pieces.

Yields 12 servings.

Szechwan Pickles

4 or 5 large cucumbers
1 tablespoon salt
4 cloves of garlic, thinly sliced
1 teaspoon Szechwan (brown) peppercorns
1 teaspoon hot bean paste
1 tablespoon hot pepper oil
2 teaspoons sugar
1 tablespoon dark Chinese vinegar
2 tablespoons sesame oil

Wash the unpeeled cucumbers. Cut into halves lengthwise and scrape out the seeds with a metal teaspoon. Cut crosswise into 1½-inch lengths, then lengthwise into pieces ½ inch wide. Mix with the salt in a large bowl. Let stand for 2 hours. Rinse and pat dry. Add the garlic, peppercorns, bean paste, hot pepper oil, sugar, vinegar and sesame oil. Marinate, covered, in the refrigerator overnight.

Yields 1 quart.

Victor Zue

In the Dark

Olive oil should always be kept in a cool, dark place. Sunlight causes oxidation, which eventually makes the oil rancid.

Yogurtlu Ispanak Ezmesi

(Spinach Yogurt Dip)

Former Host Family Program couple Gün and Dilara Keresteci introduced us to this appetizer while he was here studying for his undergraduate and master's degrees.

4 cups plain fat-free yogurt
1 (10-ounce) package frozen chopped spinach
5 large cloves of garlic, minced, or to taste
Salt to taste
½ tablespoon olive oil

Rest a mesh sieve across a dish, allowing a 2-inch clearance between the sieve and the bottom of the dish. Strain the yogurt in the sieve in the refrigerator for 12 hours or longer.

Cook the spinach using the package directions. Let cool and squeeze dry.

Combine the yogurt, spinach, garlic and salt in a medium bowl and mix well. Spoon into a medium flat dish and smooth the surface. Drizzle with the olive oil. Garnish with cayenne, paprika or sliced black olives.

Yields 18 servings.

Kate Baty

Sauerkraut Soup

1 tablespoon butter
1/2 onion, thinly sliced
4 ounces sauerkraut
4 juniper berries
1 bay leaf
2 cups meat stock
1 dried roll, cut into 1/2-inch pieces
1 tablespoon butter
1/2 cup whipping cream
Freshly ground pepper to taste

Melt 1 tablespoon butter in a stockpot. Add the onion. Cook until the onion is translucent. Reserve a small amount of the sauerkraut. Add the remaining sauerkraut, berries and bay leaf to the stockpot. Simmer over low heat for 5 minutes. Stir in the meat stock. Simmer, covered, for 15 minutes. Remove the berries and bay leaf.

Fry the bread in 1 tablespoon butter in a skillet until golden brown.

Purée the soup in a food processor or blender. Warm over low heat. Stir in the whipping cream and pepper. Ladle into bowls. Sprinkle with the croutons and reserved sauerkraut.

Yields 2 servings.

Petra Wiese

Posta en Salsa Negra

(Pot Roast in Black Sauce)

This is a typical recipe from Barranquilla, Colombia, my hometown. There are several ways to prepare this dish, but I like this way because the sauce is rich and thick, perfect for coating the slices of meat and the boiled potatoes. It is also delicious served with plain white rice.

1 medium tomato, chopped
1/2 bunch parsley, chopped
1/2 bunch scallions, chopped
1/4 cup mustard
1 teaspoon each pepper, salt and garlic powder
1 cup water
3 to 4 pounds bottom round roast
1 cup vegetable oil
Boiled potatoes (optional)

Combine the tomato, parsley, scallions, mustard, pepper, salt, garlic powder and water in a blender container. Process until mixed and pour into a large bowl. Add the roast. Marinate in the refrigerator for 2 hours to overnight, turning occasionally. Remove the roast from the marinade and pat dry. Reserve the marinade.

Heat the oil in an 8-quart pot. Add the roast and cook until dark brown. Remove the roast and discard most of the oil. Return the roast to the pot. Add the marinade. Add enough water to cover the roast halfway. Bring to a boil; cover and reduce the heat to low. Cook for 1 hour, turning occasionally. Remove the roast and let stand for 20 minutes. Cut with the grain into 1/4-inch slices. Place the slices and the potatoes in the pot. Return to a boil and cover. Cook over medium heat for 1 hour or until the roast is tender and the sauce is thick, adding additional water if needed.

Yields 10 to 12 servings.

Marta B. Ash

Sukiyaki

Chicken may be used in place of the beef in this recipe, and the vegetables may be varied according to local availability.

3 tablespoons vegetable oil
1 1/2 pounds sirloin steak, thinly sliced
2 tablespoons sugar
1/2 cup soy sauce
1/3 cup water
1 (8-ounce) can bamboo shoots, or 12 ounces bamboo shoots, sliced
1 cup thinly sliced onion
1 cup sliced celery
1 (4-ounce) can mushroom stems and pieces
1/8 teaspoon MSG
3/4 cup green onions, cut into 1-inch pieces
3/4 cup watercress, cut into 1-inch lengths

Heat the oil in a 360-degree skillet. Add the steak. Cook for 10 minutes or until light brown, stirring frequently. Mix the sugar, soy sauce and water in a bowl and pour over the steak. Bring to a boil. Cover and reduce the temperature to 220 degrees. Simmer for 40 minutes or until the steak is tender. Stir in the undrained bamboo shoots, onion, celery, undrained mushrooms and MSG. Increase the temperature to 300 degrees. Bring to a boil. Cover and cook for 5 minutes. Add the green onions and watercress. Cook, uncovered, for 1 minute, stirring constantly.

Serve at once over hot steamed rice.

You may substitute Chinese mixed vegetables for the bamboo shoots.

Yields 6 to 8 servings.

Marie Salah

Hungarian Paprika Chicken

I don't use sour cream in this recipe, but if you do, be sure to add it just before serving and heat it only for a minute.

1 1/2 pounds boneless skinless chicken breasts, chopped
1 1/2 pounds chicken thighs, deboned, skin removed, chopped
2 onions, finely chopped
3 tablespoons vegetable oil
1 tablespoon paprika
1 teaspoon salt
1 cup sour cream (optional)

Rinse the chicken and let drain. Brown the onions lightly in the oil in a skillet. Remove from the heat. Add the paprika and chicken and mix well. Sprinkle with the salt. Cover and cook over low heat for 1 hour or until the chicken is tender. Stir in the sour cream.

Yields 8 to 10 servings.

Elizabeth V. Zolnay

Chicken with Pineapple and Cashews

2 cups frozen chicken tenders, or 2 whole chicken breasts, deboned, skin removed, chopped
2 teaspoons cornstarch
2 teaspoons dry sherry
1/2 teaspoon finely chopped gingerroot
2 tablespoons soy sauce
2 tablespoons hoisin sauce
1 teaspoon sugar
2 tablespoons water
1/4 cup vegetable oil
1 clove of garlic, crushed
1 small can unsweetened pineapple chunks
1 cup blanched thinly sliced carrots
1/2 to 1 cup chopped green pea pods, green bell peppers or other green vegetable
1 cup roasted whole salted cashews

Mix the chicken, cornstarch, sherry and gingerroot in a medium bowl. Mix the soy sauce, hoisin sauce, sugar and water in a small bowl.

Heat the oil in a wok or deep 14-inch skillet over medium heat. Add the chicken. Cook for 1 to 2 minutes. Add the garlic, stirring several times. Blend in the soy sauce mixture. Add the pineapple, carrots, pea pods and cashews.

Serve over a bed of boiled rice or use rice as a side dish.

Yields 4 servings.

Kate Baty

Chicken Stir-Fry

2 tablespoons vegetable oil
1 clove of garlic, crushed
1/4 cup chopped scallions
1 pound ground chicken or turkey
2 teaspoons sugar
2 tablespoons rice wine
2 (8-ounce) cans sliced mushrooms
1 (8-ounce) can water chestnuts, chopped
2 tablespoons oyster sauce
1 teaspoon cornstarch
1/2 cup water
Chopped tofu
1 tablespoon hoisin sauce
1 teaspoon sesame oil

Heat the vegetable oil in a 12-inch wok. Add the garlic, scallions and chicken. Stir-fry until the chicken is brown. Sprinkle with the sugar. Stir in the wine. Add the mushrooms and water chestnuts. Stir in the oyster sauce. Dissolve the cornstarch in the water. Add the cornstarch mixture and tofu to the wok and mix well. Stir in the hoisin sauce and sesame oil.

Yields 4 to 6 servings.

Grace Y. Madsen

Enhancing Fresh Ginger

Store slices of ginger in a small jar of sherry. The ginger is preserved, and the flavored sherry is delicious in a Chinese stir-fry.

Pork Cooked in Tea

3 tea bags
1 pork shoulder, or 28 ounces roast pork
1 cup soy sauce
1/3 cup vinegar
2/3 cup sake
1/4 cup mirin (sweet sake)

Brew the tea bags in 4 to 6 cups water.

Tie the pork and place in a large pot. Add just enough tea to cover the pork. Cook over medium heat for 40 minutes or until the pork is cooked through.

Mix the soy sauce, vinegar, sake and mirin in a large bowl. Add the pork. Marinate in the refrigerator overnight.

Remove the pork from the marinade and cut into 1/4-inch slices. Serve cold with green lettuce, bean sprouts, sliced onions or other vegetables.

The sauce may be served on the side.

Yields 6 to 8 servings.

Keiko Kanda

Cloudy Tea

If your iced tea turns cloudy, a tablespoon or so of boiling water will usually clarify it.

Chiles Rellenos with Marinara Sauce

This dish can be prepared in the morning or the night before and baked just before serving. It will stay puffy for about five minutes–just long enough to bring it to the table!

1 (4-ounce) can California green chiles
4 ounces Monterey Jack cheese, cut into strips
4 eggs
1/3 cup milk
1/2 cup flour
1/2 teaspoon baking powder
1 cup shredded sharp Cheddar cheese
1 (15-ounce) can marinara sauce

Seed the green chiles and remove the pith. Fold or tuck the Monterey Jack cheese into the chiles. Arrange in a greased shallow 1 1/2-quart baking dish.

Beat the eggs in a mixer bowl until thick and foamy. Add the milk, flour and baking powder, beating until smooth. Pour evenly over the green chiles. Sprinkle with the Cheddar cheese.

Bake at 375 degrees for 30 minutes or until puffed and set when gently shaken.

Heat the marinara sauce in a saucepan. Garnish the rellenos with pitted black olives. Spoon onto individual plates and top with some of the sauce. Serve the remaining sauce at the table.

Yields 4 servings.

Asopao de Langosta

(Rice Stew with Lobster)

This dish is very popular in Puerto Rico. I make it for our Latin American-style New Year's Eve party.

2 tablespoons garlic-flavored vegetable oil
1/2 cup chopped onion
1/2 cup chopped green bell pepper
1 cup long grain rice
1 tablespoon capers, drained
1 (46-ounce) can chicken broth
6 cups water
1 (14-ounce) can stewed tomatoes
2 packages Sazon Goya seasoning
1 (10-ounce) can frozen lobster, 8 ounces cooked fresh lobster or 1 pound peeled deveined shrimp
Salt and pepper to taste
1 cup frozen peas

Heat the oil in an 8-quart kettle. Add the onion and green pepper. Sauté until the onion is translucent. Add the rice. Cook until brown. Add the capers, chicken broth, water and tomatoes. Stir in the seasoning. Simmer, covered, over medium heat for 45 minutes, stirring occasionally. Add the lobster. Season with the salt and pepper. Add the peas. Cook for 5 minutes, stirring frequently. Ladle into bowls. Garnish each serving with a slice of roasted red pepper and chopped cilantro.

Serve with crusty bread, a green salad and Tostones.

Yields 10 to 12 servings.

Patricia A. Bras

Tostones

(Fried Plantain)

These are everybody's favorite. When I make them, I double the recipe because everyone wants more.

3 large bright green plantains
1 teaspoon salt
Vegetable oil

Peel the plantains and slice into 1/2-inch rounds. Soak in salted water. Remove the plantains from the water and pat dry. Reserve the water.

Heat the oil in a large skillet. Add a few plantain slices; cook in batches to avoid crowding. Cook until golden yellow. Drain on paper towels. Press each slice 1/8 inch thick between 2 saucers or with a tamale maker. Dip into the salted water and pat dry. Return to the skillet. Fry until crisp but not burned.

Yields 6 servings.

Patricia A. Bras

Hungarian Cucumbers with Sour Cream

5 medium cucumbers, washed, peeled
Salt to taste
3 tablespoons vinegar
3 tablespoons water
1 1/2 tablespoons sugar
1/4 teaspoon pepper
1/2 clove of garlic, minced
1/2 small onion, finely chopped
1 cup sour cream
1/2 teaspoon paprika

Slice the cucumbers thinly into a bowl. Sprinkle with a large amount of salt; the cucumbers should taste salty. Let stand for 2 hours.

Mix the vinegar, water, sugar, pepper, garlic and onion in a bowl.

Squeeze the cucumbers dry in small batches and place in a large bowl. Pour the vinegar mixture over the cucumbers, stirring to toss lightly. Blend in the sour cream. Sprinkle with the paprika. Chill for 1 hour.

Yields 6 servings.

Elizabeth V. Zolnay

Sushi Rice

With sushi rice, you decorate with sashimi (raw fish), cooked string beans and carrots, and julienned cucumbers. Add a fried egg that has been cut into strips or slices of avocado and salmon. Even canned white meat tuna will do it!

3 cups short grain white rice
3 cups water
1 (2x4-inch) piece kombu (dried kelp) (optional)
3/4 cup rice vinegar
2 teaspoons sugar
1/2 teaspoon salt

Bring the rice, water and kombu to a boil in a saucepan. Simmer, covered, over low heat for 17 minutes. Turn off the heat and let stand, covered, for 15 minutes. Do not uncover the rice during the entire cooking process.

Mix the vinegar, sugar and salt in a bowl. Place the hot rice in a large wooden salad bowl or pasta bowl. Sprinkle the vinegar mixture over the rice, fanning constantly. Fold gently and mix until cooled.

Yields 6 to 8 servings.

Minako Wrenn

Middle Eastern Lentils with Rice

1 large onion, chopped
Vegetable oil
1 cup lentils
5 cups water
1/2 cup rice
Salt and pepper to taste

Sauté the onion in a small amount of oil in a skillet until golden brown. Cook the lentils in the water in a saucepan for 5 minutes. Add the rice. Cook for 15 minutes. Season with the salt and pepper. Turn off the heat. Let stand, covered, until all the liquid is absorbed. Spoon into a baking dish. Top with the onion.

Yields 6 to 8 servings.

Alyce McLaughlin

Vegetarian New Mexico Refried Beans

I developed this dish from a simpler dish made by my great-grandmother's cook, Pilar.

2 pounds dried pinto beans
10 quarts (about) water
2 pounds yellow or white onions, cut into quarters
3/4 cup bacon bits
1 cup vegetable oil
1 tablespoon salt
1 tablespoon dried oregano
1 teaspoon each cumin, black pepper and cayenne
1/2 teaspoon dried basil
1/2 teaspoon dried thyme
1 large bay leaf, crumbled

Sort the beans and rinse 5 times in cold water. Combine the beans, water, onions, bacon bits, oil, salt, oregano, cumin, pepper, cayenne, basil, thyme and bay leaf in a 12-quart pot. Bring to a boil over high heat. Simmer for 1 hour. Cover and simmer for 6 hours longer. Let stand, covered, in the refrigerator overnight.

Serve cold or reheat. To refry, place the mixture in a large skillet. Mash with a potato masher. Cook over low to medium heat for 2 hours or until the beans are medium brown, adding additional liquid as needed and stirring frequently with a spatula to prevent scorching.

Serve with or without sour cream, rolled up in a flour tortilla to make a burrito or as a major part of a Mexican meal!

You may substitute 1 pound chopped uncooked bacon for the bacon bits and vegetable oil.

Yields 12 servings.

Bill Orme-Johnson

Gnocchi

Delicious served with or without a sauce

2 cups warm milk
1/2 cup cream of wheat
1 teaspoon salt
1/4 cup chopped margarine
1/8 teaspoon cayenne, or to taste
1 cup shredded Cheddar cheese
1 egg, beaten

Combine the milk, cream of wheat, salt, margarine and cayenne in a double boiler over boiling water. Heat until the margarine is melted, stirring frequently. Remove from the heat. Stir in the cheese and egg. Pour into a greased casserole. Let stand at room temperature for several minutes.

Bake at 350 degrees in a pan of hot water for 1 hour or until golden brown.

Yields 6 to 8 servings.

Esther Edgerton

Adding Curry and Chili Powder

Curry and chili powder should always be added to a recipe while browning, if possible. Browning removes the bitter taste.

Knödel

(German Bread Dumplings)

These are an ideal accompaniment to braised meats, with lots of gravy.

1 pound dried Italian bread, torn into 1/4-inch pieces
2 medium onions, thinly sliced
1/2 cup unsalted butter
1/4 cup chopped parsley
Salt and pepper to taste
3 eggs, lightly beaten

Place the bread in a large bowl. Sauté the onions in the butter in a skillet until tender. Add to the bread. Add the parsley, salt and pepper and mix well. Let stand for 10 minutes. Add the eggs. Let stand for 10 minutes.

Shape the mixture into lightly packed 2-inch balls. Steam for 12 minutes. Serve immediately.

Yields 4 servings.

Nancy and Ed Hofstetter

Veal Dumplings

These veal dumplings are the low-calorie version of a high-calorie traditional German dish known as Königsberger Klopse. This version makes a light entrée in the menu, and I especially enjoy it with the small beets from New England. The side dishes are also traditional.

2 to 4 beets
1 slice toast, crusts trimmed
8 ounces potatoes, peeled
Salt to taste
8 ounces veal, ground
Chopped chives to taste
1 teaspoon mustard
1 egg
Pepper to taste
1 cup veal stock
2 tablespoons flour
2 tablespoons butter
1 tablespoon whipping cream
2 tablespoons undrained capers
1 teaspoon lemon juice
1/8 teaspoon sugar, or to taste
1 tablespoon vinegar
1 teaspoon vegetable oil
1 small onion, chopped

Cook the beets in water to cover in a saucepan until tender. Soak the toast in water to cover in a bowl. Cook the potatoes in boiling salted water in a saucepan until tender.

Drain the toast. Combine with the veal, chives, mustard, egg, salt and pepper in a large bowl. Knead until a smooth dough forms. Shape into 8 dumplings.

Drop the dumplings into the veal stock in a saucepan. Simmer, covered, for 10 minutes. Remove the dumplings. Strain the cooking liquid and set aside. Fry the flour in the butter in a skillet until golden brown. Add the cooking liquid and the whipping cream. Cook for 5 minutes, stirring constantly. Add the undrained capers, lemon juice, salt, pepper and sugar.

Mix the vinegar, oil, salt and pepper in a bowl. Peel the beets and cut into slices. Sprinkle with the vinegar mixture. Add the onion.

Reheat the dumplings in the capers sauce. Serve with the potatoes and beets.

Yields 2 servings.

Petra Wiese

Oriental Noodles

1 cup soy sauce
1 cup vegetable oil
5 cloves of garlic
Hot pepper to taste
4 sprigs of parsley
2 pounds linguini
8 ounces snow peas
1 red bell pepper, julienned
2 bunches scallions, chopped

Combine the soy sauce, oil, garlic, hot pepper and parsley in a food processor or blender container. Process until mixed.

Cook the pasta in a 4-quart pot using the package directions. Drain and return to the pot. Add the peas, red pepper, scallions and soy sauce mixture. Cook until heated through. Toss well and serve immediately.

Yields 4 to 6 servings.

Alyce McLaughlin

Chrusciki

This recipe has been modified from my mother's, which has been in the family for over seventy years. I've been making them for twenty years for Christmas. Make the dough so that it does not stick to the rolling pin. Otherwise, you will have to use too much flour to roll it out, and that will leave a residue in the oil.

3 to 4 cups flour
$1/4$ teaspoon baking powder
$1/4$ teaspoon salt
4 egg yolks
2 eggs
5 tablespoons sugar
$1/3$ cup light cream
2 jiggers rum or brandy
4 teaspoons lemon or anise extract
Vegetable oil for deep-frying
Confectioners' sugar

Mix the flour, baking powder and salt together.

Beat the egg yolks and eggs in a bowl until thickened. Add the sugar, cream, rum and flavoring and beat well. Add enough of the flour mixture to make a soft dough. Knead until the dough begins to blister. Roll $1/8$ inch thick on a lightly floured surface. Cut into $3/4$x3-inch strips.

Roll each strip very thin. Cut a 1-inch slit lengthwise in the center of 1 strip. Insert each end into the slit to form a butterfly shape. Repeat the process with the remaining strips.

Deep-fry each piece at 375 degrees until light brown. Drain on paper towels. Dust the cooled pieces with confectioners' sugar.

Yield is variable.

Chester J. Kurys

Maple Bavarian Cream

1 tablespoon unflavored gelatin
1/4 cup cold water
1/2 cup maple syrup
1 cup hot milk
1/4 cup sugar
1/4 teaspoon salt
3 egg yolks, beaten
1 teaspoon vanilla extract
1 cup whipped cream

Soften the gelatin in the cold water.

Combine the syrup, milk, sugar and salt in a double boiler. Cook over boiling water until heated through, stirring until the sugar is dissolved.

Pour a small amount of the hot mixture into the egg yolks; stir the egg yolks into the hot mixture. Cook until the mixture coats a metal spoon, stirring constantly.

Add the gelatin. Cook until the gelatin is dissolved, stirring constantly. Stir in the vanilla and let cool. Fold in the whipped cream.

Pour into a wet mold. Chill for 12 hours or longer. Unmold onto serving plate.

Yields 8 servings.

Fatima Bourass-Elzein

Middle Eastern Rice Pudding

2 quarts milk
1 cup rice, rinsed, drained
1/2 to 3/4 cup sugar
1 tablespoon cornstarch
1 teaspoon orange blossom water or vanilla extract

Bring the milk to a boil in a saucepan. Add the rice. Simmer for 20 minutes, stirring occasionally.

Stir in the sugar and cornstarch. Cook for 10 minutes or until the rice is quite tender. Stir in the flavoring before removing from the heat.

Yields 8 servings.

Nanaimo Bars

This recipe originated in Western Canada in a city called Nanaimo.

1/2 cup butter
1/4 cup sugar
1 teaspoon vanilla extract
1 egg
6 tablespoons baking cocoa
1 1/2 cups fine graham cracker crumbs
1/2 cup chopped pecans or walnuts
Flaked coconut to taste
1/4 cup butter, softened
2 cups confectioners' sugar
1 egg
4 ounces semisweet chocolate
1 tablespoon butter

Combine 1/2 cup butter, sugar, vanilla, 1 egg and cocoa in a saucepan. Cook over medium heat until light and thickened, stirring constantly. Stir in the crumbs, pecans and coconut. Press into a greased 9x9-inch dish.

Cream 1/4 cup butter in a mixer bowl until light and fluffy. Add the confectioners' sugar and 1 egg gradually, beating well after each addition. Spread over the crumb mixture. Chill for 15 minutes.

Melt the chocolate in a double boiler over hot water. Stir in 1 tablespoon butter. Spread over the confectioners' sugar layer. Chill until set. Cut into small squares.

Yields 24 servings.

Mary Catherine Birgeneau

Zabaglione with Grand Marnier

A plus with your favorite Italian dinner

6 egg yolks
2 tablespoons sugar
1/4 cup sauterne or Champagne
1 tablespoon grated orange zest
3 tablespoons Grand Marnier

Beat the egg yolks and sugar in a double boiler over simmering water until thick and pale yellow. Add the wine and orange zest. Cook until the mixture coats a metal spoon, whisking vigorously constantly. Stir in the Grand Marnier.

Serve warm or chilled over fruit or pour into parfait glasses and serve with whipped cream.

Yields 4 servings.

Prolonging Your Basket of Raspberries

Raspberries spoil very quickly. Whether hand-picked or store-bought, empty them onto a plate and sort through them, discarding any moldy ones to prevent contaminating the others. Store the good raspberries in an uncovered paper towel-lined basket or dish in the coolest part of the refrigerator. Do not wash the berries before storing, as they tend to become waterlogged. If you won't be using them within 2 days, spread the berries in a single layer on a baking sheet. Freeze on the baking sheet and then pack them into freezer bags or airtight containers.

Nanosecond Meals

(DESPERATION)

MIT
Women's League

Potage Potable

This soup is easy to make and bound to fool your guests into thinking you slaved long and hard over a hot stove to make it. A few hints: Vary spices to taste, and remember that you can't use too much sherry. In fact, if the mood strikes, forget about the soup and serve the sherry. Either way, you are bound to make an impression!

1 large can lentil soup
1 large can black bean soup
4 small red potatoes, cut into small chunks
2 medium carrots, cut into small chunks
2 cups broccoli florets
1 teaspoon coriander
1 teaspoon salt
1 teaspoon pepper
2 tablespoons Worcestershire sauce
1/2 cup sherry

Combine the soups, potatoes, carrots and broccoli in a large pot. Stir in the coriander, salt, pepper and Worcestershire sauce. Simmer, covered, until the potatoes are tender. Add the sherry. Simmer for 5 minutes.

Pour the soup into a blender container. Process until puréed, adding water or additional sherry if needed.

Serve hot with appropriate garnishes. The first name of the guest being served spelled out in sour cream on the top is a perennial favorite.

Yields 4 to 6 servings.

Jay Keyser

Cucumber and Boursin on Rye

Party rye or thinly sliced rye bread
Boursin or alouette cheese
Cucumber slices
Fresh dill to taste

Cut the rye with cookie cutters. Spread with the cheese. Top each piece with 1 cucumber slice. Sprinkle with the dill. Chill until serving time.

Yield is variable.

Quick Crab or Lobster Bisque

This is a variation of a recipe from a classmate of my mother's at Smith in 1920.

1 can tomato soup
1 can pea soup
1 can consommé
1/2 to 1 soup can sherry
7 ounces crab meat or cooked lobster
1 cup thinly sliced celery
1 cup light cream or evaporated skim milk
Salt and pepper to taste

Bring the soups and consommé to a boil in a saucepan. Add the sherry, crab meat, celery, cream, salt and pepper. Cook until just ready to boil.

Yields 6 servings.

Idella Tapley

Blintz Soufflé

½ cup margarine or butter
12 frozen blintzes, thawed
4 eggs
¼ teaspoon salt
¼ cup orange juice
⅛ to ¼ cup sugar
1 teaspoon vanilla extract
1½ cups sour cream

Melt the margarine in a 9x13-inch baking pan. Add the blintzes.

Combine the eggs, salt, orange juice, sugar, vanilla and sour cream in a blender container. Process until blended. Pour over the blintzes.

Bake at 350 degrees for 45 minutes or until golden brown.

This may be prepared the night before and refrigerated. Bake immediately before serving.

Serve with sour cream, yogurt, and strawberries or blueberries.

Yields 8 to 12 servings.

Cantaloupe and Tuna Salad

Served with hot rolls and iced tea, this makes a great desperation summertime luncheon.

1 cantaloupe
1 small can water-packed white tuna, drained
Mayonnaise
1 teaspoon (or more) curry
Chutney to taste
1 tablespoon toasted sliced almonds

Cut the cantaloupe into halves and peel. Remove the seeds.

Mix the tuna with enough mayonnaise to moisten in a bowl. Add the curry, chutney and almonds and mix well.

Fill each cantaloupe half with the tuna mixture.

Garnish with leafy lettuce and a small bunch of seedless white or red grapes.

Yields 2 servings.

Vegetable Salad

This makes a good winter salad when fresh vegetables are expensive.

1 (16-ounce) can tiny peas, drained
1 (16-ounce) can French-style green beans, drained
1 (11-ounce) can Shoe Peg corn, drained, or
  1 (15-ounce) can baby corn, drained
1/2 cup chopped sweet onion
3/4 cup chopped celery
1/4 cup chopped pimento, drained
3/4 cup sugar
1/2 cup salad oil
1/2 cup white wine vinegar or cider vinegar
1/2 teaspoon salt
1/4 teaspoon pepper

Combine the peas, green beans, corn, onion, celery and pimento in a 2-quart bowl and mix well.

Combine the sugar, oil, vinegar, salt and pepper in a 1-quart saucepan. Cook over medium heat until heated through, stirring until the sugar is dissolved. Pour over the vegetable mixture.

Let cool. Cover and refrigerate overnight.

This keeps for several days in the refrigerator, and it travels well.

Yields 10 servings.

Bette Ritz

Scalloped Chicken

1 (16-ounce) package herb-seasoned stuffing mix
3 to 5 cups chopped cooked chicken
1/2 cup margarine or butter
1/2 cup flour
1/4 teaspoon salt
1/8 teaspoon pepper, or to taste
4 cups seasoned broth, cooled
6 eggs
1 (10-ounce) can cream of mushroom soup
1/4 cup milk
1 cup sour cream or plain yogurt
1/4 cup chopped pimento

Prepare the stuffing using the package directions. Spread in a baking pan. Top with the chicken.

Melt the margarine in a large saucepan. Blend in the flour, salt and pepper. Add the broth. Cook until heated through. Stir a small amount of the hot mixture into the eggs; stir the eggs into the hot mixture. Cook until thickened, stirring constantly. Pour over the chicken.

Bake at 325 degrees for 45 minutes. Let stand for 5 minutes.

Mix the soup, milk, sour cream and pimento in a bowl. Serve hot or cold over the baked chicken mixture or on the side.

Yields 8 servings.

Elsa Buchannan

Oriental Chicken Bake

This is a great, easy way to prepare delicious chicken. It makes a wonderful sandwich for a picnic in the country or on your favorite beach.

2 pounds boneless skinless chicken breasts, cut into smaller pieces
2 tablespoons curry powder
2 tablespoons soy sauce
1/2 cup Dijon mustard
1/2 cup honey

Rinse the chicken and pat dry.

Place the chicken in a roaster or shallow pan. Mix the curry powder, soy sauce, Dijon mustard and honey in a bowl. Pour most of the mixture over the chicken, reserving several spoonfuls. Let stand for several minutes.

Bake at 350 degrees for 1 hour or until the chicken is golden brown and cooked through, turning once and basting with the reserved honey mixture.

Serve hot or cold.

Yields 6 to 8 servings.

Chicken Spenser

This is an expanded version of a meal described in one of Robert Parker's Spenser detective novels, which are set in Boston. Spenser is a very tough guy but happens to enjoy cooking, especially for his longtime friend Susan. The basis of this recipe is described in some detail in a scene in which Spenser prepares the marinated chicken and chops the vegetables, takes some time off for a romantic interlude with Susan, and then finishes the meal and serves it to her with a crisp white wine (by candlelight, I'm sure). I have added to and changed some of the vegetables, but it's still good with a crisp white wine and candles!

1 boneless chicken breast, split into halves
1 teaspoon rosemary
1/4 cup olive oil
1 tablespoon lemon juice
1/4 cup chopped onion
1/2 cup chopped broccoli
1/2 carrot, thinly sliced
1 clove of garlic, crushed
2 tablespoons olive oil
1 teaspoon tarragon

Sprinkle the chicken with the rosemary. Mix 1/4 cup olive oil and lemon juice in a bowl. Add the chicken. Marinate, covered, in the refrigerator for 30 minutes or longer.

Sauté the onion, broccoli, carrot and garlic in 2 tablespoons olive oil in an 8-inch skillet for 5 minutes. Sprinkle with the tarragon. Remove the vegetables and keep warm. Add additional olive oil to the skillet if needed. Add the chicken. Cook for 3 to 4 minutes per side or until cooked through.

Combine the chicken and vegetables in a serving dish. Serve with rice or pasta.

Yields 2 servings.

Katherine H. Strehle

Chicken and Broccoli Casserole

1 cup rice
2 whole chicken breasts, deboned, split into halves
Freshly ground pepper (optional)
1/2 cup chopped onion
1 (20-ounce) package frozen chopped broccoli, thawed
1 (10-ounce) can cream of mushroom soup
1 cup shredded Swiss cheese
1/4 cup chicken broth

Prepare the rice using the package directions.

Coat the chicken with the pepper. Cook in a skillet sprayed with nonstick cooking spray for 20 minutes or until browned. Add the onion. Cook for 10 minutes.

Place the rice in a 2-quart casserole sprayed with nonstick cooking spray. Add the broccoli and the chicken mixture. Pour a mixture of the soup, cheese and broth over the chicken.

Bake, covered, at 350 degrees for 35 to 40 minutes or until heated through. You may top with bread crumbs and bake, uncovered, during the last 5 minutes of baking time.

Yields 4 servings.

Katherine Allen

"Fried" Spaghetti

Northern Italian housewives who were caught without staples for the family meal would put the pasta on the stove to cook while they ran out to the henhouse to search for eggs. It took little else but Parmesan cheese to complete the meal. This dish is very tasty, and it can be made with 2 to 6 eggs, depending on the level of desperation, using more Parmesan with fewer eggs and/or less Parmesan with more eggs. If cholesterol is a concern, an egg substitute can be used with only a slight loss of flavor. The recipe was passed down from both my grandmothers, one of whom was born in Italy, the other being a first-generation American.

8 ounces spaghetti, linguini or vermicelli
4 eggs
1/4 cup grated Parmesan cheese
Salt and pepper to taste
1 tablespoon olive oil

Cook the pasta in boiling salted water in a 10-quart pot using the package directions.

Beat the eggs in a bowl. Add the cheese, salt and pepper and mix well.

Drain the pasta. Heat the olive oil in a large skillet. Add the pasta. Stir in the egg mixture. Cook until the eggs are the desired degree of doneness, stirring constantly.

Serve immediately with a green salad and/or crusty bread.

Yields 3 to 4 servings.

Maryann Goblick

Spaghetti with Clam Sauce

2 (7-ounce) cans minced clams
1/4 cup olive oil
2 cloves of garlic, minced
8 ounces spaghetti or linguini
Chopped parsley or chives (optional)

Drain the clams, reserving the liquid.

Heat the olive oil in a skillet. Add the garlic. Cook for 4 minutes or until golden brown. Add the reserved liquid. Cook until reduced by 1/4 to 1/2. Stir in the clams just before serving. Arrange the spaghetti on individual plates. Spoon the sauce over the spaghetti. Sprinkle with the parsley.

Serve with white wine, salad, crisp bread and fruit.

Yields 2 to 3 servings.

Joan and Rich Sasiela

Sugar Variations

Be aware that not all sugars are created equal. The recent addition of dextrose by some sugar manufacturers can alter the end product in cookies, candies and other baked goods. Read the labels, and avoid dextrose when possible.

Tuna Pasta

1 (6-ounce) can chopped clams
8 ounces bacon, cut into 1/2-inch strips
1 clove of garlic, crushed
1/2 cup sliced black olives
1 or 2 cans water-packed white tuna, flaked
2 tablespoons olive oil or butter
8 ounces pasta, cooked, drained
3 tablespoons chopped parsley

Drain the clams, reserving the liquid.

Cook the bacon in a skillet over low heat until crisp. Remove the bacon and drain the skillet. Add the garlic, clams, black olives and tuna to the skillet. Stir in the olive oil. Cook until heated through.

Combine with the pasta in a bowl and toss well. Stir in a small amount of the reserved liquid and/or additional olive oil. Arrange on individual plates. Sprinkle with the parsley and garnish with lemon wedges.

Yields 4 servings.

Dee Ippen

Scallops

Cornmeal
Flour
Salt and pepper to taste
8 ounces scallops
2 tablespoons olive oil
1/2 cup vermouth
Chopped Italian parsley

Mix the cornmeal, flour, salt and pepper in a shallow dish. Coat the scallops lightly with the mixture.

Sauté the scallops quickly in the olive oil in a skillet. Remove to a warmed dish. Add the vermouth and parsley to the skillet, stirring to deglaze the skillet. Pour over the scallops.

Serve over brown rice or mixed brown and white rice.

Yields 2 to 3 servings.

Dorothy Dahl

Longer-Lasting Firm Whipped Cream

Place your whipping cream, sugar, vanilla and beaters in a bowl in the refrigerator for at least 30 minutes before whipping. Your whipped cream will stay firm much longer.

Graham Cracker Brittle Cookies

I have served this several times with coffee at Travel Club meetings. People do not detect the graham cracker base, and they always ask for the recipe as it is a bit "different!"

24 graham crackers, separated into halves
1 cup butter
1/2 cup sugar
1 cup broken walnuts, pecans or almonds

Place the graham crackers in an 11x13 inch nonstick baking sheet with sides.

Melt the butter in a saucepan. Stir in the sugar. Bring to a boil over medium heat, stirring constantly. Cook for 2 minutes, stirring constantly. Stir in the walnuts. Pour over the graham crackers.

Bake at 350 degrees for 10 minutes or until bubbly but not too brown. Separate the pieces a bit as it begins to cool. Remove to a wire rack to cool completely. Store in an airtight container.

Serve with tea in the afternoon, with morning coffee or as a small snack.

Yields 20 servings.

Frances P. Elliott

Rum Cake

1 (2-layer) package pudding-recipe yellow cake mix
Dark rum
1/2 cup butter
1/4 cup water
1 cup sugar
1/2 cup dark rum

Prepare the cake mix using the package directions, substituting dark rum for half the water. Pour into a nonstick bundt pan. Bake at 325 degrees for 35 minutes or until the cake tests done. Cool in the pan for several minutes. Invert onto a large plate with a rim.

Melt the butter in a saucepan. Stir in the water and sugar. Boil for 5 minutes, stirring constantly. Remove from the heat and stir in 1/2 cup rum.

Pierce the cake several times with a wooden pick. Drizzle the rum mixture over the cake.

Yields 16 servings.

Donna Coveney

Shortcake

1½ cups sifted cake flour
1 teaspoon baking powder
⅛ teaspoon salt, or to taste
½ cup milk
1 teaspoon vanilla extract
1 tablespoon butter, softened
¾ cup sugar
1 egg

Sift the flour, baking powder and salt together. Mix the milk and vanilla in a bowl.

Cream the butter and sugar in a mixer bowl until light and fluffy. Beat in the egg. Beat in the flour mixture and milk mixture alternately, beginning and ending with the flour mixture. Pour into a greased and floured 8- or 9-inch cake pan.

Bake at 350 degrees for 25 minutes or until the cake tests done.

Serve with strawberries or blueberries.

Yields 6 to 8 servings.

Bette Ritz

Swedish Walnut Cake

Have your guests try to guess the secret ingredient!

2 eggs
2 cups sugar
1 (20-ounce) can crushed pineapple
2 cups sifted flour
2 teaspoons baking soda
1 teaspoon vanilla extract
½ cup chopped English walnuts
8 ounces cream cheese, softened
½ cup butter, softened
1¾ cups confectioners' sugar
1 teaspoon vanilla extract
½ cup chopped English walnuts

Combine the eggs, sugar, undrained pineapple, flour, baking soda, 1 teaspoon vanilla and ½ cup walnuts in a bowl and mix well. Pour into a greased 9x13-inch cake pan. Bake at 350 degrees for 40 minutes.

Combine the cream cheese, butter, confectioners' sugar and 1 teaspoon vanilla in a bowl and beat until of a spreading consistency. Spread over the cooled cake.

Sprinkle with ½ cup walnuts.

Yields 15 servings.

Food Affinities

Basil has long been an essential ingredient in Italian cooking. Its spicy taste has always been associated with dishes that contain tomatoes, pesto, veal stuffing, and cottage cheese mixtures. Try purple basil in pale celery soup, salads, and rice dishes for color, texture, and a pungent spicy surprise.

Chives are a subtle substitute for onion. Choicest are the white flowering garlic chives; they are less common and add a hint of garlic to food. Either type can be used when onion is called for. As they leave no aftertaste, chives are an excellent alternative for people who cannot eat onion or garlic.

Dill is a multi-purpose herb that should not be thought of only in relation to pickles. Use dillseeds to flavor beets, fish sauces, and potato salad. Dillweed can be added to fish, eggs, green beans, on top of broiled tomatoes, or on soft cheese mixtures. Dill bread is wonderful!

Marjoram (sweet) is delicious with squash, veal dishes, poultry and game stuffings, gravies, chicken salad, or vegetable salads. Use marjoram in a multitude of dishes but always with discretion—its odor and flavor can be persuasive.

Mint is overused in toothpaste, chewing gum, cigarettes, and commercial sauces and jellies for lamb. However, don't give up on mint. This herb can be so refreshing in teas, salads, drinks, and fruits. Try it on peas, carrots, and boiled potatoes and in dressing for fish.

Oregano is another essential herb in Italian cooking. This herb can be used interchangeably with sweet marjoram.

Parsley should ***not*** be used simply as a garnish. Buy both curly and Italian long-leaf and eat it! Parsley is full of nutrition. Deep-fry large sprigs; throw it freely into cream sauces, gravies, stews, and soups.

Rosemary can be rubbed into the surface of duck, pork, or lamb before roasting. Mix rosemary with horseradish for fish sauce. It is perfect in dressings for citrus fruit salads, and it adds a subtle flavor to jams and sweet sauces.

Sage is not just for turkey stuffing. Use it subtly in beef and sausage mixtures. It gives a lovely flavor to soft cheeses, wild duck, goose, and boiled onions in cream sauce.

Summer savory is traditionally coupled with snap beans. It adds a somewhat smoky flavor to dishes made from dried peas, hot or cold beans, lentil soup, and meat and poultry stuffing.

Tarragon (French) is, of course, used in classic French sauces, but it also has an affinity with seafood, egg dishes, mushrooms, chicken, sweetbreads, and aspics.

Thyme (French) is one of the traditional herbs in a bouquet garni (the others being bay leaves and parsley) and is used in many vegetables (it's especially good in carrots with sweet butter), soups, meats, and breads.

Most herbs can be substituted one for another, so be creative! Don't just think of tarragon with chicken and dill with fish—instead try basil and mint and enjoy!

—slightly adapted with permission of the authors from the New England Unit of The Herb Society of America, Inc.

CHARTS

Equivalents

When the Recipe Calls For	Use
Baking	
$\frac{1}{2}$ cup butter	4 ounces
2 cups butter	1 pound
4 cups all-purpose flour	1 pound
$4\frac{1}{2}$ to 5 cups sifted cake flour	1 pound
1 square chocolate	1 ounce
1 cup semisweet chocolate chips	6 ounces
4 cups marshmallows	1 pound
$2\frac{1}{4}$ cups packed brown sugar	1 pound
4 cups confectioners' sugar	1 pound
2 cups granulated sugar	1 pound
Cereal-Bread	
1 cup fine dry bread crumbs	4 to 5 slices
1 cup soft bread crumbs	2 slices
1 cup small bread cubes	2 slices
1 cup fine cracker crumbs	28 saltines
1 cup fine graham cracker crumbs	15 crackers
1 cup vanilla wafer crumbs	22 wafers
1 cup crushed cornflakes	3 cups uncrushed
4 cups cooked macaroni	8 ounces uncooked
5 cups rolled oats	1 pound
$3\frac{1}{2}$ cups cooked rice	1 cup uncooked
Dairy	
1 cup shredded cheese	4 ounces
1 cup cottage cheese	8 ounces
1 cup sour cream	8 ounces
1 cup whipped cream	$\frac{1}{2}$ cup heavy cream
$\frac{2}{3}$ cup evaporated milk	1 small can
$1\frac{2}{3}$ cups evaporated milk	1 (13-ounce) can
Fruit	
4 cups sliced or chopped apples	4 medium
1 cup mashed bananas	3 medium
2 cups pitted cherries	4 cups unpitted
$2\frac{1}{2}$ cups shredded coconut	8 ounces

When the Recipe Calls For	Use
Fruit (continued)	
4 cups cranberries	1 pound
1 cup pitted dates	1 (8-ounce) package
1 cup candied fruit	1 (8-ounce) package
3 to 4 tablespoons lemon juice plus 1 tablespoon grated lemon peel	1 lemon
$\frac{1}{3}$ cup orange juice plus 2 teaspoons grated orange peel	1 orange
4 cups sliced peaches	8 medium
2 cups pitted prunes	1 (12-ounce) package
3 cups raisins	1 (15-ounce) package
Herbs	
1 tablespoon chopped fresh herbs	1 teaspoon dried herbs
Meats	
4 cups chopped cooked chicken	1 (5-pound) chicken
3 cups chopped cooked meat	1 pound, cooked
2 cups cooked ground meat	1 pound, cooked
Nuts	
1 cup chopped nuts	4 ounces shelled 1 pound unshelled
Vegetables	
2 cups cooked green beans	$\frac{1}{2}$ pound fresh or 1 (16-ounce) can
$2\frac{1}{2}$ cups lima beans or red beans	1 cup dried, cooked
4 cups shredded cabbage	1 pound
1 cup grated carrot	1 large
8 ounces fresh mushrooms	1 (4-ounce) can
1 cup chopped onion	1 large
4 cups sliced or chopped potatoes	4 medium
2 cups canned tomatoes	1 (16-ounce) can

MIT CHARTS

Food Storage

Get the most out of your ingredients by storing them in the proper places. Here is some advice on how to keep your cooking necessities fresh and flavorful.

Baking Powder: Store the airtight tins in a cool, dry place and replace every 6 months.

Baking Soda: Store in an airtight container in a cool, dry place for about 6 months.

Beans: Once a package is opened, dry beans should not be refrigerated but stored in airtight containers in a cold, dry, dark place. They will keep for about 1 year.

Brown sugar: Store brown sugar in a tightly covered container for up to 4 months.

Chocolate: Store chocolate for no longer than 1 year. It should be kept in a cool, dry place with a temperature range of 60° F to 75° F. If the storage temperature exceeds 75° F, some of the cocoa butter may separate and rise to the surface, causing a whitish color to the chocolate called "bloom."

Dried fruit: Store unopened packages of dried fruit in a cool, dry place or in the refrigerator. Store opened packages in an airtight container in the refrigerator or freezer for 6 to 8 months.

Flour: Store flour in a clean, tightly covered container at room temperature for up to 1 year.

Garlic: Garlic should be stored in a dry, airy place away from light.

Granulated sugar: Store sugar in a tightly covered container for up to 2 years.

Greens: It is best to place unwashed greens in a plastic bag in the refrigerator and wash them just before using. If it is necessary to wash the greens before storing, wash and dry them well, preferably in a salad spinner. Store them in sealable plastic bags in the refrigerator.

Nuts: For optimum freshness and shelf life, nuts should be stored, preferably unshelled, in a tightly covered container in the refrigerator or freezer and shelled as needed. (The shell and the cool temperature keep the nut from turning rancid.)

Poppy seeds and sesame seeds: Fresh poppy seeds and sesame seeds should be kept in airtight containers in the refrigerator so they will not become rancid.

Potatoes: Potatoes, as well as other root vegetables, keep well in a dark, cool place, preferably a cellar. Store them in a dark brown paper bag.

Shredded coconut: Store in a cool, dry place in an airtight container. Do not store in the refrigerator.

Yeast: Store in the freezer or refrigerator in a closed plastic bag.

MIT

Photography Index

Photo on page 58 by Lincoln Laboratory, MIT

Photo on page 134 by The MIT Museum

All other photos by Donna Coveney, *Tech Talk*, MIT

MIT

Index

MIT

INDEX

INDEX

MIT

INDEX

For additional copies of
What's Cooking Under The Dome
send $20.00 to:

MIT Women's League
77 Massachusetts Avenue
Cambridge, Massachusetts 02139
Tel: (617) 253-3656

Copies may be purchased at the League office or directly from League members for $15.95 each.

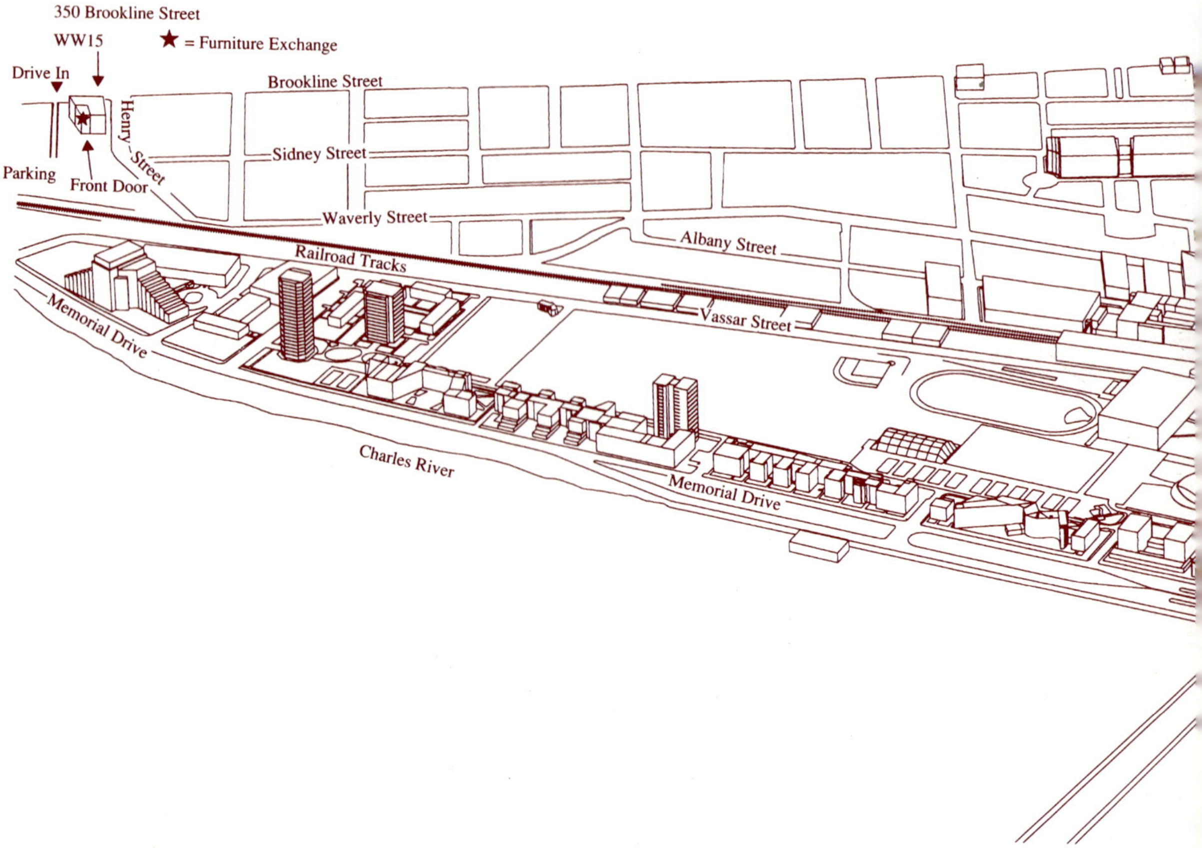
350 Brookline Street
WW15
★ = Furniture Exchange
Drive In
Parking
Front Door
Brookline Street
Henry Street
Sidney Street
Waverly Street
Albany Street
Railroad Tracks
Vassar Street
Memorial Drive
Charles River
Memorial Drive